First Edition

TRUE LOVE & SEXUAL INTIMACY

In A Christian Marriage

*How To Give Your Spouse Unconditional Love
And Mind Blowing Ecstasy*

JOSSY PHIRI

Copyright © 2020 Jossy Phiri

All rights reserved.

ISBN - 9789982180573

Published by Unipress Zambia Ltd,
Telefax: +260 211 226815, **Cell:** +260 977874921
Email: sales@unipresszambia.com/josphiri@yahoo.com

www.unipresszambia.com

TABLE OF CONTENTS

DEDICATION

VERONICA PHIRI

This book is dedicated to my beautiful wife and soul mate, **Veronica Phiri**, the most amazing person ever, my lover, and best friend, with whom I share a happy and enjoyable marriage. Thank you for being a great blessing and source of encouragement to me and our children. Your love for God is amazing. May God continue to shower you with his blessings and joy unspeakable in Jesus' name. May He increase and enlarge your sphere of influence. I love you dearly.

ACKNOWLEDGEMENTS

In my first act as an author, I would like to honour my **Lord and Savour Jesus Christ** for saving me and giving me the ability to write this book.

I would like to express my profound gratitude to a great icon and spiritual leader of our time, **Bishop Dr. Joe Imakando**, the presiding Bishop of Bread of life Church International, and our mother **Reverend Bernadette Imakando** for being a great inspiration to couples and source of wisdom and valuable spiritual guidance.

Pastor Dr. Andrew Kumwenda and his dear wife, thank you for your encouragement.

I would like to acknowledge **Dr. Chipepo Lombe Chibesakunda,** who agreed to do a foreword to this book and added flavour to this publication. I can't thank you enough, not in a million years. As an apposite medical expert your contribution and level of understanding of the human biology espoused in this book is much appreciated. Indeed science investigates but the Bible interprets. Last but not the least, I would like also to acknowledge my dear Pastor friend and true brother, **Dr. Kenny Mwansa** from **SplendidWorks,**

- For Media Consultancy,
- Page-Layout,
- Cover Design and
- Editing of this book.

You are truly a rare gem. Without your passion and commitment to your duty, this book would have taken long to publish. May the God we serve together bless you immensely.

The principle of choice is our yard stick of choosing to love our spouse in spite of their shortcomings.

SYNOPSIS

The main theme and emphasis of this book is to help people understand what an ideal Christian marriage is in modern day society.

However, it would be a total lie if I claimed to have written this book without consulting other people's scholarly works.

I therefore, wish to acknowledge my indebtedness to the numerous authors of both offline and online dictionaries, books, and other publications, which I consulted.

I am extremely grateful to all friends for their support, encouragement and suggestions towards this book. A big thank you to all those who helped to edit and typeset this book.

My wife and I, have been marriage counselors in Bread of Life Church International for more than 17 years now. In our tenure of office we have counseled a substantial number of couples who are happily married even to date. It is with this background that I was prompted in my spirit to write this book so that many married couples can experience true love and fulfilling sexual intimacy in their marriages.

Therefore, when writing this book I had three categories of people in mind; the first group is the newlyweds, those with no marital experience whatsoever. Those who kept themselves pure in their singlehood without involving themselves in premarital sex. But a few months after getting married they become frustrated, confused and resentful because their expectations about an ideal marriage become an illusion. The second category comprises those that have been married for quite a number of years. They bore children, but still unable to find fulfillment in their marriage.

The third category comprises a few couples that have been happily married for years, but still need valuable marital knowledge to enable them consolidate the gains so as to avoid any pitfalls in marriage.

FOREWORD

Dr. Chipepo L. Chibesakunda

Scripture declares, **"Wisdom is the principal thing, therefore get wisdom. And in all your getting, get understanding"**.

Proverbs 4:7 NKJV

In a world where there are so many voices and opinions about marriage, from tradition, culture, social media etc., navigating through all of it as a couple can be pretty daunting!

If you're one of those couples I have good news for you, fear not! God's word admonishes us that as we go about getting to different levels and stages in our lives (which includes getting married) that we should get understanding.

Why would God ask us to get understanding?

Because wisdom is the principal thing. **"True love and Sexual intimacy"** is a comprehensive compilation of great wisdom for all categories of married couples. **Elder Jossy Phiri's 27 years of being married and 17 years of being a marriage counselor enriches each and every page of this book with not only his personal experience but also an extraordinary understanding of love and**

intimacy. This book is not your everyday ordinary guide on marriage but it's a profound exposition that details every aspect of our being (physically, socially, emotionally and spiritually) in order that the reader may understand the depth of love and sexual intimacy.

As a medical doctor I'm excited about Elder Jossy's book because of how meticulously he has broken down every aspect of what healthy relationships should look like from the psychology to the anatomy. Phiri reminds us that we are intricate beings, with different aspects that come together as one in order to function well. Therefore there's need to take all aspects into consideration in relationships in order to experience the fullness of love and sexual intimacy. He candidly describes the human body and how it relates to sexual intimacy and takes the reader through a step by step description of all the aspects of love and sexual intimacy.

He surely has left "no stone unturned!" You're guaranteed nothing less than an extraordinary journey that will lead to exponential growth in your knowledge and understanding of love as you read through. **The timing of this book couldn't be better, as the wisdom it contains is very much relevant and needed to help married couples for such a time as this!**

Dr. Chipepo L. Chibesakunda

True love in a marriage
relationship is characterized by
upholding these virtues;
Commitment, Selflessness,
Sacrifice, Patience, Discipline,
Kindness, and Forgiveness.

Agape love is the unconditional love that transcends human understanding or reasoning. Its translation is love in the verb-form: It is demonstrated by your behaviour towards another person.

INTRODUCTION

True Love and Sexual Intimacy in marriage is a book that seeks to help married couples unlock and rediscover the secretes and techniques of true love and sexual intimacy in marriage as God originally intended it to be.

However, a huge number of married couples have been struggling for years trying to find the real meaning of true love and sexual fulfillment in marriage. It seems true Love and Sex has been so elusive to married couples that many have been left deranged. Some married couples have never known what it is to be in true love. Most of them have very sad, painful and traumatic marriage experiences. They have memories which are filled with frustration and resentment towards marriage. Many married couples have spent more than half of their life without experiencing true love and the ultimate sexual pleasure. Some married women don't even know what an orgasm is, because they have never experienced one before. Yes, they don't know what it is to be in real love and enjoying true intimacy in marriage. Others have been barely hanging on to marriage because of the children they have.

As a matter of fact, true love and sexual pleasure in marriage can be an illusion and a farfetched dream without the involvement of the one who instituted marriage. The actual master key to true love and sexual pleasure in marriage is the Lord Jesus Christ himself. He alone is the only answer to true peace, harmony and maximum sexual pleasure in marriage. There is no marriage which can flourish without letting our Lord Jesus Christ take centre stage. Therefore the first and most important thing for any couple to do is to allow our Jesus Christ be Lord over their marriage. Hence, the need for both husband and wife to surrender their lives to the Lord. The Holy Scriptures says that,

"Behold, I stand at the door and knock. If anyone hears my voice and opens the door, I will come in to him and dine with him, and he with me." **Revelation 3: 20.**

This is the starting point of recovery and restoration of grappling marriages. Without first acknowledging and inviting the Lord Jesus Christ in our hearts and accepting him as our lord and personal Saviour, there will be no peace in our homes. Without the saving knowledge of our Lord Jesus Christ-abuse of marriage is inevitable. There is no peace in such marriages and it's impossible to enjoy true love and sexual intimacy.

We cannot do without God because He is the creator and originator of marriage. Therefore He is the only master key to true love and sexual pleasure in marriage. He knew why He said , "it was not good for man to be alone"; and out of the man's rib He made a woman to be his companion. It is therefore unwise not to involve God in marital issues because He is the one who ordained the institution of marriage. He has given us the life giving manual (The Bible) with reliable instructions to make marriage work.

The sole purpose of the devil is to steal, kill and destroy marriages. Satan does this by hiding the liberating truth of the word of God by isolating a couple from having an intimate relationship with God the father and the only source of true love and sexual pleasure in marriage. We shouldn't allow the devil to take centre stage of marriage. The moment we do so, God's best plan for marriage will be hijacked and perverted to suit the devil's wicked schemes.

As a matter of fact, my heart goes to the newlyweds and other married couples that have been shaped over the years by the traditional belief that almost all household chores in a home must be done by a woman. However, this belief and custom is counterproductive in modern day society were household chores must be shared accordingly between husband and wife.

In our Zambian culture in particular, it is a custom cutting across all tribes. This custom has been entrenched in our society. Especially in so called 'polygamous' marriages, most married women are forced to work in fields. On the other hand, in some section of society it is considered a taboo for a married man to cook, sweep, wash, and do other household chores. There is no true love and genuine sexual intimacy in such marriages. It is high time this custom and belief was abolished or done away with.

My wife and I, were not exceptions to this custom and belief. Actually, when I married my wife on 31st May, 1992, we were young and naïve with no marital experience whatsoever. I had built a house right at my parent's plot. This made the life of my wife as a newlywed unbearable. Actually, the first three years of our marriage were characterized by pain due to lack of knowledge.

She would wake up early in the morning to fetch water. During the week she would often accompany my mother to work in the field. When going back home later in the day she would carry a heavy load of firewood on her head. As soon as she arrives home, she would usually start preparing food for the family. She had actually no time to rest and enjoy marriage. I was completely oblivious to what was going on because I was also indoctrinated with the wrong custom and belief (that a married woman should do all house chores in a home and her husband should just sit and relax).

Who said that a husband can't cook, bake, wash the dishes, prepare the bed, sweep, fetch water, clean the surrounding, water the lawn, bath children, wash clothes, iron clothes, work in the field, feed the baby, put the baby to sleep, and all other house chores? If you have enough income at your disposal you can employ a maid, garden boy and other essential workers so that you and your wife have enough time to relax, romance and enjoy yourselves. I am not saying that wives should not engage themselves in productive work in a home. However, what I'm trying to put across is that wives are human beings as well and not machines. Regardless of the fact that they are wives, they also need enough time to rest.

In fact I had no idea of how to affectionately love and cherish a woman. I didn't realise the damage I was causing to her physically, mentally and emotionally. This mental and psychological torture led to a breakdown in her physical health. From nowhere, my wife started fitting and biting her tongue uncontrollable. This ordeal was traumatizing both to my wife and I. Her condition deteriorated with time. We were frequently in and out of hospital. This was strange to us because there was no history of epilepsy in her family.

What helped us was our strong faith in the Lord. We realized that this terrible condition needed God's intervention. In our confusion and pain, we sought the face of God through prayer and fasting. It was not until in 1996 when we started attending couples seminars organized by Bread of Life Couples Ministry that our marriage got totally revolutionized. One of the main speakers during these meetings was the late **elder Mutwale** and his late dear wife

–(May their souls rest in eternal peace). It was also during the same year 1996 that my wife was miraculously healed during an Easter Conference at Bread of Life Church International in Emmasdale, Lusaka, Zambia. What a mighty God we serve! To Him be all the glory.

In fact, what has impacted us greatly over the years is the effectual ministry of the word of God by our father in the Lord **Bishop Dr. Joe Imakando** and our mother, **Rev. Bernadette Imakando**. We have benefited immensely through their wise marital counsel and teachings. It is with this background that the dream of seeing strong, happy, healthy, and successful marriages was birthed. Hence, if you desire to truly love and give your spouse satisfying sexual intimacy, then this book is a must have because it is meant for you.

CHAPTER ONE

TRUE LOVE AND SEX IN
MARRIAGE

TRUE LOVE-THE HEARTBEAT OF MARRIAGE

WHAT IS LOVE?

The meaning of LOVE according to - www.merriam Webster.com

LOVE - Noun:

1 a (1)   Strong affection for another arising out of kinship or personal ties – maternal love for a child

(2)   Attraction based on sexual desire: affection and tenderness felt by lovers after all these years, they are still in love.

(3) Affection based on admiration, benevolence, or Common interests.

LOVE: verb

1. To hold dear: CHERISH

2. a. to feel a lover's passion, devotion, or tenderness for

    b. (1): caress

       (2): to fondle amorously

       (3): to copulate with

DEFINITION FOR LOVE: The meaning of LOVE according to the -English language learners dictionary;

LOVE - Noun

: a feeling of strong or constant affection for a person.

: attraction that includes sexual desire

: the strong affection felt by people who have a romantic relationship

: a person you love in a romantic way

LOVE - Verb

: to feel great affection for (someone)

: to feel love for (someone)

: to feel sexual or romantic love for (someone)

: to like or desire (something) very much

: To take great pleasure in (something)

DEFINITION OF LOVE: The meaning of LOVE according to the Oxford English Learners dictionary;

LOVE: Love is a strong feeling of deep affection for somebody or something, especially a member of your family or a friend: a mother's love for her children, love between blood sister and brother.

LOVE: As a strong feeling of affection for somebody that you are sexually attracted to: especially between a husband and wife.

THE FOUR TYPES OF LOVE

The four types of love in the Greek are; Storge, Philia, Eros and Agape. Find below the definition of each type of love:

STORGE: Storge love is an affectionate love. This is the type of love that one might have for a family member or friend. This is the love that a mother naturally exhibits for her child. It is the love that family members feel for each other. The love that friends feel for each other. This type of love if not checked may lead into a romantic relationship for friends of the opposite sex. It is also Love for one's country or kindred. Mostly it occurs naturally without any coercion.

PHILIA: Philia love is a brotherly kind of love often exhibited in a close friendship. It is warm and tender platonic love meaning that it does not involve itself in sexual activities. A good example of Philia love is the love exhibited between David and Jonathan in the Bible (1 Samuel 18:3). Despite you having Agape love for your enemies, you may not exhibit Philia love for the same kind of people.

EROS: It is a passionate and romantic sexual love. Eros is a Greek word and it is a source of an English word called erotic. Eros love is very important in a marriage relationship because it is intended to arouse or stimulate sexual feelings. It can easily be abused and mostly mistaken for storge love.

AGAPE: Agape love is the unconditional love that transcends human understanding or reasoning. Its translation is love in the verb-form: It is demonstrated by your behaviour towards another person. It is actually the God kind of love. It is sacrificial in nature as well as giving and expecting nothing in return. In fact, it is more than just a feeling, but an act of the will. It accepts the object of love regardless of their flaws, shortcomings or faults. This is the type of love that every married couple should strive to have for their fellow spouse. Even though you may not like their behaviour, you choose to love them just the way they are. As a matter of fact, this is the highest form of love amongst the four types of love.

"For God so loved the world that He gave His only begotten son, that whoever believes in Him should not perish but have everlasting life." John 3:16

"For He made him who knew no sin to be sin for us, that we might become the righteousness of God in Him." 2 Corinthians 5:21

A good example of Agape love is better illustrated through the parable of the prodigal son. Although the prodigal son led a sinful and wasteful life, after repentance the father welcomed him as a beloved son. (Luke 15:11-32).

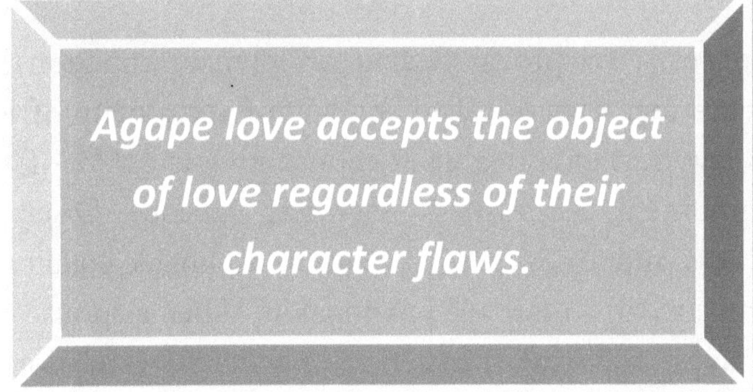

TRUE LOVE IN MARRIAGE

Love is a feeling of intense attraction towards someone. This implies that there is gravitation towards the object of love. Furthermore, it implies that the object of love is precious to behold because it is an embodiment of true inner beauty. It is a wonder to behold, adorned with beauty a sum total of both outward and inner true beauty which is a priceless virtue. Hence the adage, 'beauty is in the eye of the beholder' because it is only the beholder who appreciates the object of love.

Therefore, if both the husband and wife gravitate towards each other because of the chemistry between them, then the equation of true love is complete. This is the golden rule of love.

"Therefore, whatever you want men to do to you, do also to them…" Matthews 7:12 NKJV.

It creates a reciprocal feeling of intense attraction in a couple's life. This is called the law of reciprocity of love. This law demands that each spouse invests 100% of their Commitment, Selflessness, Sacrifice, Patience, Discipline, kindness, and forgiveness to create a sustainable equilibrium of true love in a marriage relationship. When a spouse does not invest 100% of themselves in a marriage relationship then it will be impossible to maintain a sustainable equilibrium of true love. However, the deficit can be compensated by choosing to love anyhow despite the other spouse not keeping the other end of their bargain.

True love is a choice. A choice is an act of choosing between two or more possibilities; something that you can choose. Therefore, you can either choose to love or not to love someone. This is the power that you have at your disposal-the power of choice. At almost every given moment in our lives, we are faced with options to choose from. Every day, life will present options to us whether good or bad and it is up to us to make a wise choice.

Actually, before you got married, life had presented to you a broad spectrum of choices-the people to choose from for a life partner-husband or wife. And out of more than 7.8 billion people globally you had the courage to choose your life partner. You had a set of criteria of requirements to help you make the right choice.

As a matter of fact you have no excuse not to love your spouse despite them not living up to their promise. The bible says that for God so loved the world that he gave His only begotten son so that whosoever believes in Him should not perish, but have eternal life. Our Lord Jesus Christ kept the end of his bargain despite us failing to do so. The Holy Scriptures says that while we were yet sinners Christ died for us. He demonstrated his love for us by dying a painful death on the cross of Calvary, so that whosoever believes in

Him should not perish, but have everlasting life. He came to his own, but his own did not recognize him.

"So ought men to love their wives as their own bodies. He that loveth his wife loveth himself. For no man ever yet hated his own flesh; but nourisheth and cherisheth it, even as the Lord the church: For we are members of his body, of his flesh, and of his bones. For this cause shall a man leave his father and mother, and shall be joined unto his wife, and they two shall be one flesh. This is a great mystery: but I speak concerning Christ and the church. Nevertheless let every one of you in particular so love his wife even as himself; and the wife see that she reverence her husband." Ephesians 5:23-33

THE SEVEN CHARACTERISTICS OF TRUE LOVE IN MARRIAGE

God is Love. He is the embodiment of True Love. The agape Love. The unconditional kind of Love. The characteristics of true love and most important attributes to a sustainable loving marriage relationship are as follows: Commitment, Selflessness, Sacrifice, Patience, Discipline, Kindness, and Forgiveness. True love in a relationship can only be actualised by upholding these attributes or values. These characteristics are what define the real meaning of true love in a marriage or any other relationship.

"Love suffers long and is kind; love does not envy; love does not parade itself, is not puffed up; does not behave rudely, does not seek its own, is not provoked, thinks no evil; does not rejoice in iniquity, but rejoices in the truth; bears all things, believes all things, hopes all things, endures all things." 1 Corinthian 13:4-7

1.) LOVE IS COMMITMENT

COMMITMENT: Commitment is to be completely loyal to a person or spouse, a thing and pledge to devote all your time and effort to fulfilling set objectives and plans.

You cannot claim to be in true love when you fail to commit yourself hundred percent to a marriage relationship. There is no true love without commitment. Commitment is a vital characteristic of true love.

True love is commitment, meaning that regardless of any difficulties, challenges, friction or differences you might be facing as a couple in your marriage, you remain loyal to each other. Commitment will determine the successful landing of your marriage relationship despite the turbulence in the flight of life. Commitment does not give up despite many challenges in your marriage relationship. Commitment will cause you to embrace each other despite the pain of betrayal from your spouse.

Actually what causes more pain to a spouse is the thought of being misunderstood by someone they love the most. Someone you trust so much. Most of the time we expect good treatment and a good listening ear from our beloved ones. However, we tend to be misunderstood no matter how hard we try to explain ourselves. Our explanation sometimes falls on deaf ears. Who else can vindicate us if our very own beloved partner is planning to end the marriage in divorce. In times like this we need to look to God for our vindication and deliverance. This is the time of reckoning when true love for our spouse is tested. How can you forgive someone who is failing to understand you and is not showing any signs of love towards you, in whose sight you are already judged/condemned.

Nevertheless, true love is total commitment to a married partner regardless of his/her short comings. True love is action oriented, it is putting the interest of the object of love before self. It doesn't withhold or deny the spouse an opportunity to enjoy their legal rights, but ensures that those rights are duly given without any reservation.

Feelings come and go, but true love, a commitment to another person, perseveres and ultimately conquers all. When you have been offended let love lead. You should choose to take positive and not negative action towards the object of your love. Love is a commitment that conquers all things. With commitment and persistence you can actually have depth in warm feelings of true love.

No matter how difficult and turbulent the journey of married life might be, don't lose hope and direction, but remain resolute and true to the promise you made on your wedding day. "In sickness and in healthy, until death do us part.

Commitment is what makes a couple stick together despite facing numerous marital challenges. Commitment is the gear that keeps marriage running. Without commitment marriage will go nowhere. Remember, you publicly made a vow to remain loyal to your partner for life. Commitment will see you through even in old age. Despite you losing all your teeth due to old age, and when the glory of your youth diminishes. Commitment will cause you to reach the finishing line strong. Aging with sufficient grace.

> **Show Me A Couple That Is Experiencing True Love And Sexual Intimacy, Then I Will Show You A Couple That Is Truly Committed To Their Marriage Relationship.**

The moment you said I do to your partner you literally made a declaration of lifelong commitment to marriage. As a husband you commit to love her, protect her, provide for her and meet her sexual needs for life. To the wife the declaration of commitment simply means that you will submit to him, respect him, be his companion, and meet his sexual needs for life. You pledge and commit to forsake all others and embrace your spouse as your top priority.

Joseph is a good example in the Bible, he made a vow and lifetime commitment to serve the Lord, such that when he was pressured to sleep with Portfar's wife, he stood his ground and remained true to his commitment. He was carrying great destiny to deliver his family from famine. And eventually became the Prime Minister of Egypt and a conduit or link for the Messiah to be born.

Are you going to remain true to your commitment to love your spouse for life? When things get tough will you still remain by his or her side? The choice is yours. Commitment is what gets the job done. Commitment is what makes marriage successful. Commitment is the gear of marriage. Show me a committed couple then I will show you a focused couple. A couple that doesn't get easily distracted by false accusations against them from people who wish to see them fail or throw in the towel.

"A Commitment is what transforms a Promise into reality."
Abraham Lincoln

"Without Commitment You cannot have depth in anything Whether it's a Relationship, a Business, or a Hobby." Neil strauss

"Without Commitment, nothing happens." T.D. Jakes

"Commitment leads to Action. Action brings your dreams closer."
Marcia Wieder

2.) LOVE IS SELFLESSNESS

SELFLESSNESS: Selflessness in the context of marriage is the ability to think more about the needs and happiness of your spouse than yourself.

You cannot claim to be in true love when you fail to exhibit selflessness towards your beloved spouse. There is no true love without selflessness. Selflessness is the characteristic of true love. This entails that in your action you exhibit kindness and generosity unlike being selfish or self-centered. You put your spouse's interests, happiness and wellbeing first. While the opposite of selflessness is being preoccupied by self: what is in it for me: What are my benefits: my total gain in marriage. Self-Centeredness led to the fall of Satan (Lucifer), as shown in the following scripture Isaiah 14:12-17. The Bible says;

"How you are fallen from heaven, O Lucifer, son of the morning! How you are cut down to the ground, You who weakened the nations! For you have said in your heart: 'I will ascend into heaven,

I will exalt my throne above the stars of God; I will also sit on the mount of the congregation on the farthest sides of the north; I will ascend above the heights of the clouds I will be like the Most High.' Yet you shall be brought down to Sheol, To the lowest depths of the Pit." Isaiah 14:12-17

However, a good example of selflessness is our Lord Jesus Christ, the Bible says and I quote;

"Let this mind be in you, which was also in Christ Jesus: Who, being in the form of God, thought it not robbery to be equal with God: But made himself of no reputation, and took upon him the form of a servant, and was made in the likeness of men: And being found in fashion as a man, he humbled himself, and became obedient unto death, even death of the cross." Philippians 2:5-8.

In pursuit of a loving and sexually fulfilling lifelong marriage relationship, self-denial and prioritizing your spouse's interests, happiness, and wellbeing is key.

When husband and wife compete with each other all the time at becoming the best lover ever by looking for best possible opportunities to do good or senseless acts of kindness to each other, then a dream of true love and sexual fulfillment in marriage will become a reality. True love and intimate sexual fulfillment in marriage is a manifestation of selflessness on the part of husband and wife. Actually, an atmosphere which is already pregnant with true love will automatically trigger an ultimate sexual fulfillment. Such an atmosphere makes lovemaking easy.   No wonder, before having sexual intercourse a couple should always seek to reconnect intimately at a deeper level through an act of lovemaking.

When you put your partner's interest first and look for best possible ways or opportunities to provide selfless acts of kindness and service to them, then secretes of true romance and sexual fulfillment in your marriage will become a reality.

3.) LOVE IS SACRIFICE

SACRIFICE: Sacrifice is giving up something of value or importance to you in order to get or pursue something that seems more important and of great value.

Your spouse is priceless and very valuable to you. He/she is worth sacrificing for. If you love something dearly, you will be able to sacrifice for it. You cannot claim to be in true love if you fail to sacrifice yourself for the sake of your beloved spouse. There is no true love without sacrifice. Sacrifice is the characteristic of true love. Sacrifice is denying yourself of immediate pleasure by investing your seed into a profitable venture to be realized in the future. Sacrifice is delayed gratification. Sacrifice is to choose to endure pain now and enjoy later. Love is not love until you take risk by sacrificing your life for it.

If your goal in marriage is to pursue a happy and enjoyable marriage relationship that ensures an ultimate true love and sexual fulfillment, then sacrifice is the key to realizing this dream. There is no sweet without sweat. There is actually no success without sacrifice. Marriage is no exception, sacrifice is the only road to success. Sacrifice is choosing to live with your spouse despite their inadequacies-when you know that your spouse is unable to conceive or maybe has a low sperm count. It is when your husband has been declared redundant at his work place, but you choose to remain committed to him.

Find below some tips on how best you can make your marriage successful through sacrifice:

> **Time:** Choose to sacrifice valuable time on your marriage relationship. Spend more valuable/quality time with your spouse. Remember, your spouse ought to be your best companion. In your daily schedule set aside enough time to be with your spouse. Remember when you choose to sacrifice your valuable time on your marriage, what literally you are doing is replenishing your marriage for more love and intimate sexual fulfillment.

> Learn to sacrifice financial resources in your relationship. Take a vacation and buy your spouse a valuable gift. Learn to spoil your significant other. Sacrifice by buying books on true love and sexual pleasure in marriage.

> Let go of retrogressive friendships that work against your marriage. It will be a painful decision but it's worth it. In marriage you often sacrifice your wishes by settling for a win, win situation. At times you win by losing.

LOVE IS NOT LOVE
UNTILL YOU TAKE A
RISK BY SACRIFICING
YOUR LIFE FOR IT.

4.) LOVE IS PATIENT

PATIENCE: Is the ability to remain calm and not become agitated or annoyed when your expectations are delayed. You endure pain as you await for the manifestation of your blessings. Patience is the mother of expectation. When dealing with issues and difficult situations patience will guarantee victory. Patience is love. Be patient with your spouse because he/she is not perfect yet. You cannot claim to be in true love when you fail to exercise patience with your beloved spouse. There is no true love without patience. Patience is the characteristic of true love.

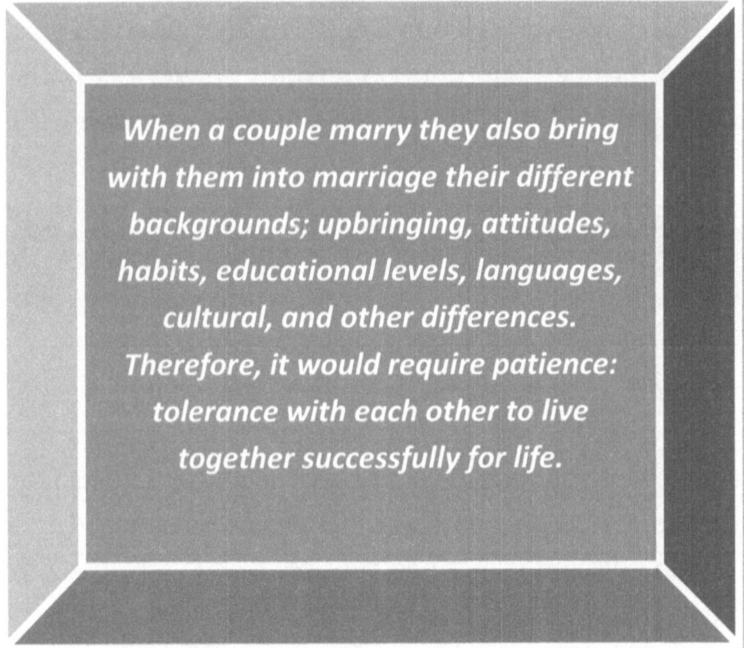

Since each spouse is different from the other they need to create enough room for tolerance. Don't force your spouse to change overnight, but with patience the necessary adjustments can be done gradually to meet your aspirations as a couple. Stop condemning your wife that she is not a good cook. If she is not then teach her or better still take her to school so that she can get an education in cooking. Love is patient so be patient with her, she is your companion and not a slave. There is great potential in her, so invest in her dearly by making sure that the untapped potential in her is actualized to the maximum. Make her a better person than you first met her.

We have a proverb in our language Chichewa/Chinyanja, which says that "kuona maso ankhono nkudekha mtima" meaning **that if you are to see the eyes of a snail then you have to exercise some patience.** If you become impatient it will be impossible for you to see the snail's eyes, because the moment you make some noise it withdraws and hide itself in its shell. It's a proverb which teaches us about the importance of patience if we are to achieve much in life. It is good to be patient with yourself and others especially your spouse. In case you have been offended by someone's behavior or conduct learn to be patient with them. Don't throw the baby out with the bathwater, meaning that we shouldn't discard something valuable along with something not wanted. We may not like someone's eating habits, but this shouldn't be the reason for one to divorce a spouse.

With patience and tolerance a spouse's eating habits can change over time and later become a great blessing in your life. Actually, many people may admire a particular couple that is happily married and doing very fine in life. However, if you inquire about their background you will discover that with patience and tolerance with each other they have matured to be the fantastic couple they are today. Rome was not built in one day. You too with patience and perseverance you will certainly achieve great success in life.

"Patience is the key element of success." - Bill Gates

5.) LOVE IS DISCIPLINE

DISCIPLINE: Is defined as control gained by enforcing obedience or order.

The Root and Meanings of Discipline; Discipline comes from discipulus, the Latin word for pupil, which also provided the source of the word disciple (albeit by way of a Late Latin sense-shift to "a follower of Jesus Christ in his lifetime"). Given that several meanings of discipline deal with study, governing one's behavior, and instruction, one might assume that the word's first meaning in English had to do with education. In fact, the earliest known use of discipline appears to be punishment-related; it first was used in the 13th century to refer to chastisement of a religious nature, such as self-flagellation. (Merriam - Webster Dictionary)

Discipline is essential if our marriages are to experience true love and sexual fulfillment. You cannot claim to be in true love when you fail to live a disciplined life with your beloved spouse. There is no true love without discipline. Discipline is the characteristic of true love.

You need to take an introspective look into your own life to see what you need to change and improve for yourself. You need to realise that you have a very big role to play in fostering positive change in your marriage. You normally choose your own thoughts and actions and sometimes those thoughts and actions are not only detrimental for your spouse but also to you as an individual too. You need to get rid of bad habits which are detrimental to your marriage. Like someone who needs to amputate a gangrenous limb to prevent death, you need to identify what parts of your personality and mindset are rotting and, even though it's painful, cut it off from yourself. Only you can change yourself. Discipline is the true mark of greatness. It's only a disciplined athlete who is destined to win. Only you can change yourself. Discipline is the true mark of greatness.

> *Only you can change yourself. Discipline is the true mark of greatness. It's only a disciplined athlete who is destined to win.*

It's only a disciplined athlete who is destined to win. True love and sexual fulfillment in marriage is a product of a disciplined lifestyle. When a couple lacks discipline unhappiness becomes a certainty in their marriage. What are the qualities of a disciplined lifestyle in marriage?

- Self-discipline gives you the power to stick to your decisions until all your goals have been achieved.

- Self-discipline gives you self-control

- It is the attitude of doing the right thing at the right time without being forced

*"Do you not know that those who run in a race all run, but one receives the prize? Run in such a way that you may obtain it, and everyone who competes for the prize is temperate in all things. Now they do it to obtain a perishable crown, but we for an imperishable crown. Therefore I run thus: not with uncertainty. Thus I fight: not as one who beats the air. But I discipline my body and bring it into subjection, lest, when I have preached to others, I myself should become disqualified." **-1 Corinthians 9:24-27***

6.) LOVE IS KINDNESS

You cannot claim to be in true love when you fail to show kindness to your beloved spouse. There is no true love without kindness. Kindness is the characteristic of true love.

KINDNESS: Is the ability or quality of being gentle and considerate of other people's feelings and wellbeing. It is treating people with respect and dignity. Therefore, true love is kindness because love can never be love without showing kindness to your lover. Even though you have been wronged you are still expected to treat them with respect and honour because true love doesn't keep records of wrong doings.

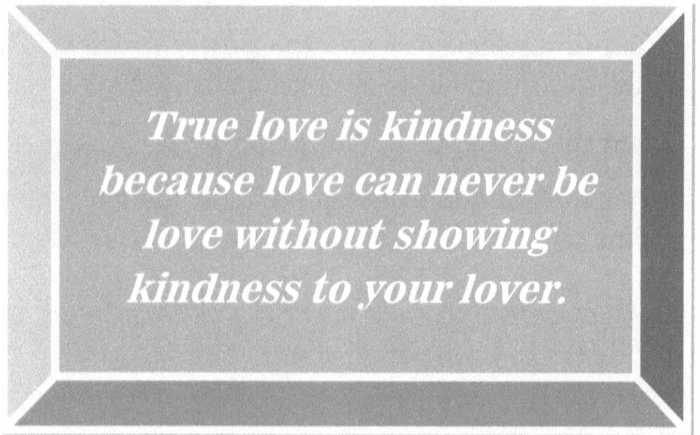

When you say you love your spouse and yet you mistreat them badly over trivial issues, insult and abuse them verbally, beat them up, threaten to kill them and take away their freedom to enjoying their basic human rights. If you deny them access to the provision of food, decent shelter, and clothing so as to punish them then you are not exhibiting true love.

7.) TRUE LOVE IS FORGIVENESS

FORGIVENESS: Is the act of forgiving. To forgive is to cease to feel resentment against an offender.

You cannot claim to be in true love when you fail to forgive your beloved spouse. There is no true love without forgiveness. Forgiveness is the characteristic of true love. Human beings are emotional beings, which means that at any given time our feelings can be hurt or exhilarated by our spouse knowingly or unknowingly. Our actions can either make our spouse feel happy or sad. It is therefore our responsibility to seek forgiveness when we realise that we have hurt someone's feelings. When we are sad it implies that we have been grieved by the loss of something valuable or offended by either our own or someone else's misconduct. However, forgiveness of either yourself or your perceived enemies sets you free from the bondage of unforgiving and gives you power to start afresh in a relationship and recreates a new future of new possibilities for both you and your spouse to explore. Unforgiving is a prison to oneself which sees no hope for the future.

> **It is always honourable to agree to disagree and respect each other's opinions.**

If someone fails to forgive himself/herself they become possessed with the spirit of anger and rage which can lead them to contemplate ending their own life and that of their partner by committing murder and suicide. This is the case of Cain and Abel in the bible. Cain was filled with the spirit of unforgiving and resentment towards his innocent young brother whose offering was accepted by God while his was rejected.

"And in the process of time it came to pass that Cain brought an offering of the ground to the Lord. Abel also brought of the first born of his flock and of their fat. And the Lord respected Abel and his offering, but He did not respect Cain and his offering. And Cain was very angry, and his countenance fell. So the Lord said to Cain, "Why are you angry? And why has your countenance fallen? If you do well, will you not be accepted? And if you do not do well, sin lies at the door. And its desire is for you, but you should rule over it." Now Cain talked with Abel his brother; and it came to pass, when they were in the field, that Cain rose up against Abel his brother and killed him." **Genesis 4:3-8.**

When we fail to forgive and allow hatred and resentment in our hearts the end result will be disastrous. We shouldn't allow the spirit of anger and rage to control us to the point of committing murder or suicide.

Imagine a situation where one kills his/her own beloved spouse and takes his/her own life because they couldn't forgive or resolve their differences amicably.

> *Forgiveness of either yourself or your perceived enemies sets you free from the bondage of unforgiving and gives you power to start afresh in a relationship and recreates a new future with new possibilities for both you and your spouse to explore.*

It is always honourable to agree to disagree and respect each other's opinions. Committing murder is barbaric and demonic of its worst kind. This is also the case of Judas Iscariot in the Bible who committed suicide when he failed to seek forgiveness and embrace a new start in life after betraying our Lord Jesus Christ over a few pieces of coin.

THE THREE ESSENTIAL ELEMENTS OF A SUCCESSFUL MARRIAGE

LOVE, SEX AND TRUST

The three most important elements of a successful marriage namely: Love, Sex and Trust. In the absence of these three elements marriage can hardly function successfully.

The three most important elements that sustain human life on this planet are namely; Air (Oxygen), water/ food, and land.

Can marriage exist without love, sex and trust? Well, love, sex and trust are essential elements of a happy and enjoyable marriage. These three elements constitute the lifeblood of an ideal marriage.

Love is like oxygen we breathe in. No human being can live without oxygen for more than 3 to 10 minutes. After three minutes without oxygen brain cells begin to die. Sex is like water or food to life. No human body can live without water for more than three days, and no one can survive for three weeks without food.

> *For any human being on this planet to survive or exist actually needs the support of air, water/food and land. In the same vein marriage can hardly exist without love, sex and trust.*

Trust is like land. Land guarantees the existence of human life. Imagine a planet without land. How can human beings be supported without land. Land is essential for human existence here on earth.

You can't have human life without air, water/food and land. Life is dependent on air/oxygen, water, food and land. For any human being on this planet to survive or exist actually needs the support of air, water/food and land. In the same vein marriage can hardly exist without love, sex and trust.

Trust is the bedrock or foundation of a strong and successful marriage. Similarly, the stronger and deeper the foundation, the taller and larger the building will be. In other words, a strong and deeper foundation will determine the size and strength of the building. The taller and larger the building is the stronger and deeper the foundation is supposed to be.

> *Trust is the bedrock or foundation of a strong and successful marriage. Similarly, the stronger and deeper the foundation, the taller and larger the building will be.*

There is a correlation between the depth and strength of the foundation and the ultimate size, lifespan and strength of the building. Therefore, trust is critical to the survival and development of a marriage relationship. The human body is supported by the backbone, so without the backbone it is impossible for the human body to be held together. So trust is the backbone that holds marriage together. Trust is the foundation of marriage. Without a strong foundation a building cannot stand the test of time.

Love is the oxygen that we breathe in, and sex is the water or food that sustains a marriage relationship. Love is the oxygen of marriage, Trust is the backbone of marriage and Sex is an indispensable water or food of marriage. When one is deprived of oxygen suffocation sets in and death is inevitable.

Love, sex, and trust create an ideal environment for marriage to flourish and achieve its intended goals and objectives. Love, sex, and trust make it possible for the main goal and objective of marriage to come to fruition. That is to provide companionship between husband and wife, and to ensure the propagation or continuity of the human race. Therefore, love, sex, and trust provide a legal framework for the ultimate consummation of marriage and fulfillment of God's mandate to populate the earth and subdue it. Love, Sex, and trust are vital components of any marriage relationship. These components ensure the healthy and success of any marriage relationship. Hence, any marriage relationship can't be successful devoid of love, sex, and trust.

LOVE - THE OXYGEN OF MARRIAGE

> ***LOVE is the oxygen that sustains marriage. Without the flow of the oxygen of love, the existence of marriage is threatened to its very core. LOVE is a breath of fresh air to a healthy and successful marriage.***

LOVE: Is the oxygen that sustains marriage. Without the flow of the oxygen of love, the existence of marriage is threatened to its very core. **LOVE** is a breath of fresh air to a healthy and successful marriage. What you need as a couple is a breath of fresh air of love. A Husband ought to be a breath of fresh air of love to his wife. Equally a wife ought to be a breath of fresh air to her husband.

This creates an ideal environment for marriage to flourish. An environment which is not hostile, but peaceable and friendly. It fosters growth and development, but in the absence of love an ugly face of animosity manifests, and when it does it leaves a trail of destruction behind. We have heard of stories of murder in our neighborhood involving married couples. Such acts of horror happen due to lack of true love in marriages.

This usually happens when we neglect the need to nature true love, harmony and peace in our homes and also ignore the channels of communication. Instead, we allow love to be contaminated by toxic elements such as anger, resentment, rage and frustration. Whenever we notice emotions of hate, anger and rage fuming in our midst we should quickly address such without hesitation. The channels of communication are vital for the survival of our marriages hence the need to leave them open at all times. Therefore, don't allow a situation where your breath of fresh air of love becomes toxic. Toxic air is deadly and very dangerous because it doesn't support life. I urge you as a couple to guard and cherish this vital element of love-oxygen in your marriage. It is very important for your marriage survival and enjoyment.

Don't allow a situation where the breath of fresh air in your marriage is polluted or contaminated with impurities or toxic elements such as infidelity, mistrust, quarrelling, fighting, conflict, insults, hate, anger, resentment, bitterness, lack of forgiveness, malice, slander, backbiting, frustration etc. If your spouse is a fresh breath of air of love, you can't subject him/her to a life of torture, insults, disrespectful, beatings, but to a life of respect and dignity because your joy and happiness revolves around them. The Bible says that love your neighbour as you love yourself. Therefore, it is mandatory to love your spouse as you love yourself. If you abuse or torture your spouse, then you are torturing and abusing yourself because your survival revolves around the very partner you are mistreating.

The moment one inhales the breath of fresh air (oxygen) every essential organ of the body is revived or renewed as it receives a new lease of life. Let us make sure that we become a blessing and not a curse to our spouse' wellbeing. It doesn't matter how badly you have been hurt by the conduct of your spouse, don't cease being a blessing to them. Don't stop to bear good fruit in season and out of season. Instead, let your breath of fresh air of love continually be purified until it reaches a level of purity of perfect love; the God kind of love which is unconditional. Free from any toxic elements. This dimension of love is a standard which every couple should aim for.

> *Let your breath of fresh air of love continually be purified until it reaches a level of purity of perfect love; the God kind of love which is unconditional. Free from any toxic elements. This dimension of love is a standard which every couple should aim for.*

Husbands ought to love their wives unreservedly. The God kind of love which is unconditional: Agape Love. The love that gives and gives and gives without holding back. This love doesn't get tired. It doesn't give up easily in spite of any mountain of offense or obstacle along the way. It is quick to let go of any malice, slander, anger, bitterness, resentment, and ready to embrace forgiveness.

Husbands need to take note of the fact that a woman is a weaker vessel, therefore it is the responsibility of every man to see to it that a woman is handled with great care and love, with the God kind of love called agape Love. This is one of the most important needs of a woman which ought to be met by the husband alone and not any other person. Once met it will eventually lead to a higher dimension of intimacy called romantic love which culminates into sexual union.

SEX IS THE WATER OR FOOD OF MARRIAGE

SEX is that chilled drinking water that quenches the fires and passion of a sexually thirsty soul in marriage. Sex is the delicious food that satisfies a sexually aroused spouse. Without sex there is no marriage. SEX is not only meant for procreation to populate the earth, but also for enjoyment between husband and wife. It is the water or food to a couple for a nourished, healthy and happy marriage.

A Good and satisfactory sex encounter is like taking a chilled glass of drinking water to quench the fires and passion of a thirsty and desperate soul. A desperate, restless and sexually aroused spouse won't rest until he/she drinks of the waters of sex or eats a delicious meal of sex.

Thirsty for water or hunger for food. The moment the water is drank or taken there is peace unspoken and total contentment of the soul because all the fires of sexual passion dies down to a relaxation of calmness. It is the nutritious and delicious food of marriage. If any plant is to grow healthily and bear much fruit then a nutritious food is required. Therefore, if any marriage is to grow healthily and produce much fruit then the nutritious and delicious food of sex is indispensable. The moment you deny your spouse of this much needed nutritious and delicious food of sex then starvation sets in and your marriage is likely to suffer from malnutrition. Sex starvation in marriage is unwarranted for. You have a huge responsibility as a couple to ensure that you don't deprive each other of sex. Regardless of the fact that women generally take long for them to be aroused sexually, it doesn't necessarily mean that they don't enjoy sex. Naturally women differ from men in terms of their responsiveness to sexual arousal. On the other hand, the responsiveness of men to sexual arousal is very quick unlike women. Despite women's sexual responsiveness being very slow, once aroused it is very easy for them to go on and experience as many orgasms as possible. Every woman has a great responsibility to see to it that her husband is kept satisfied sexually. A sexually satisfied man is usually at peace with himself, his wife and his surroundings, but a sexually starved man is like a thirsty man looking for cold and chilled water to quench his thirst. Sexual satisfaction is one of the most important needs of man which can only be met by his wife and not any other person.

TRUST-THE BEDROCK OF MARRIAGE

Trust is the bedrock of a healthy and successful marriage relationship. Trust is a prerequisite in any meaningful relationship or partnership. Therefore trust in a marriage relationship means firm belief in the reliability of your spouse/partner as an authentic, genuine, honesty, dependable and truthful person in character/behaviour at all times. Trust is an expensive virtue which should never be traded with anything. So if you think of cheating on your spouse think again, because it is very difficult to restore trust once broken. Trust makes you feel safe to open up and share your life with your spouse physically, spiritually and emotionally.

Trust is the bedrock/foundation of marriage. You choose to be vulnerable to your spouse in pursuit of a lifelong happy romantic relationship. Mind you, your spouse is not perfect like an angel, but human with weaknesses and deficiencies, and has the inherent capacity to offend, injure and disappoint you at any time.

Without trust, it will certainly be impossible to realise marriage's full potential. Equally, if trust is not established in a relationship prior to marriage, a couple is setting itself up for a disastrous future. Hence the need for young people who intend to marry to keep their virginity until that day when declared husband and wife. Trust is having faith in your partner. Trust in marriage entails that you take a risk by entrusting your life to your spouse, believing that you won't be hurt through mistrust or betrayal. Therefore, marriage should be built on mutual trust and respect.

Trust is usually earned over time. It is certainly much more difficult to earn trust back when broken. Therefore, it is imperative to safeguard yourself and your spouse from the devastation and pain of broken trust. Find below some tips to help maintain trust in your marriage;

ACCOUNTABILITY: Take keen interest in the life of your spouse. Allow your spouse to have access to your confidential information such as email accounts, phone records and financial documents to help create accountability and responsibility. Transparency in marriage keeps both husband and wife in check.

"The heart is deceitful above all things, And desperately wicked; who can know it?" **Jeremiah 17:14**

HONESTY: Honesty is the best policy in marriage, meaning that it is always good to tell the truth than a lie. So if a spouse is caught up in an extra marital affair it is in the best interest of both partners to tell the truth unlike keeping it as a secret or pretending as though all is well. If left unchecked the wayward spouse will end up in a cobweb of a deep, more involving, passionate and extra marital sexual relationship. But when disclosed or discovered early most spouses will not only forgive, but will help you work through your situation. Don't allow shame and guilty to lock you in. Being honest about things with your spouse allows you to join and help your partner find a way out of that challenging situation.

"An excellent wife, who can find? For her worth is far above jewels, The heart of her husband trusts in her, And he will have no lack of gain. She does him good and not evil All the days of her life." **Proverbs 31:10-12**

Trust is the bedrock of a healthy and successful marriage relationship. Trust is a prerequisite in any meaningful relationship or partnership.

CHAPTER TWO

THE IMPORTANCE OF EFFECTIVE COMMUNICATION IN MARRIAGE

No marriage is insulated from conflict. Remember that you never married an angel, but a saved sinner like yourself and it takes two to tangle (dance) or make an argument. However, the issue is how do you settle conflicts in marriage as soon as they arise?

You cannot claim to be in true love when you fail to effectively communicate with your spouse. There is no true love without effective communication. Communication is key to true love and sexual intimacy in marriage. Successful and effective communication within marriage is key to a happy and enjoyable union. Lack of proper communication in marriage can lead to breakdown of the rule of law and order. Which means that without quick intervention marriage can turn into a war zone and eventual dissolution.

Learn how to effectively communicate to each other as a couple. Sometimes, just being there, it is a good communication in itself. Effective communication in marriage is the most important key to a happy and successful relationship. If used and applied correctly effective communication can help a couple enjoy true intimacy and avoid bad experiences of frustration, anger and resentment.

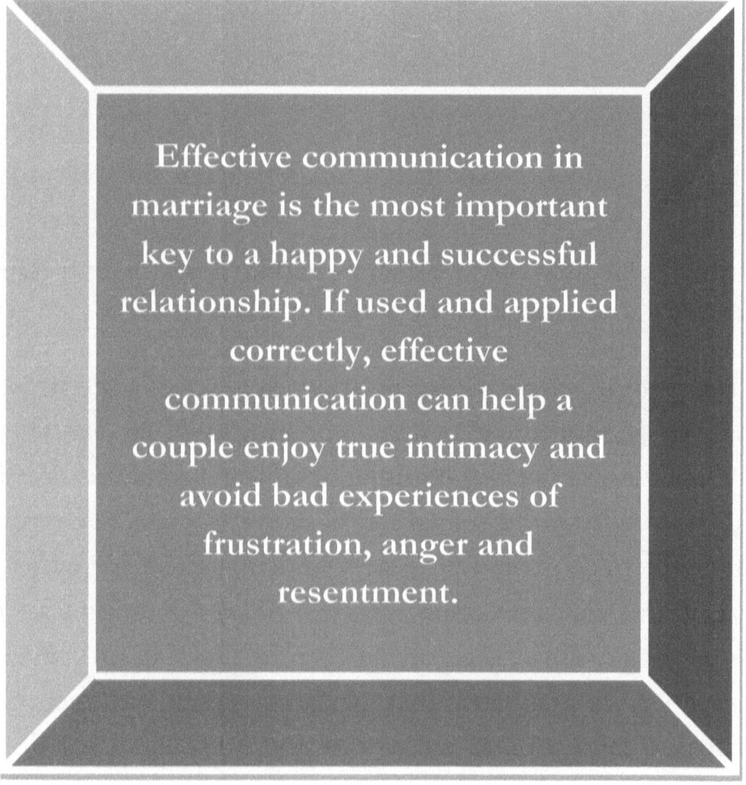

COMMUNICATION: Is a process by which information is exchanged between individuals through verbal and non-verbal medium. Verbal or spoken medium of communication include (tone of voice, volume, and pitch). Non-verbal or unspoken medium of communication include (facial expressions, gestures, body movement/language (kinesics), timing, touch, body posture, physical distance between communicators (proxemics), written and visual medium.

PURPOSE: Basically, the whole purpose of verbal and non-verbal communication is for both the sender and recipient to accurately convey and interpret the message or information and give accurate feedback. And the whole purpose of written and visual communication is for the sender to accurately encode (to change ordinary language into letters, symbols, etc. in order to send secret messages), and also for the receiver to decode (to find the meaning of something, especially that has been written in code) and give accurate feedback to the sender.

VERBAL COMMUNICATION

Verbal (Spoken or oral) Communication may include the tone of voice, volume, and pitch. The tone of voice, volume and pitch matter a lot when talking to your spouse. In order to avoid conveying a wrong message to your partner try by all means to tone down your voice and speak in a calm manner. You should as well learn not to speak on top of your voice as though you have a quarrel with your spouse. In a nutshell, learn to reduce or tone down the volume of your voice when speaking. The pitch of your voice matters a lot as well so ensure not to speak on a high pitch, but maintain a low one. For example, when you quarrel as a couple you tend to raise the tone of your voice and mercilessly shout at each other. If you both raise the volume and pitch of your voice no one will be ready to listen to the other. Actually, if you allow pride to dictate your emotions, your marriage will suffer irreparable damage. In such circumstances no one will image the winner.

NON-VERBAL COMMUNICATION

Non-verbal Communication include Facial Expressions, gestures, body movement, language (kinesics), timing, touch, body posture, physical distance between communicators (proxemics), written and visual medium.

It is estimated in some circles of society that 70 - 80% of communication is non-verbal. Non - verbal communication usually compliments spoken or oral communication. Actually, additional information and meaning can be clearly conveyed through non-verbal signals.

As a couple you should always pay much attention to non-verbal signals as you relate to your spouse. These signals could convey beneficial profound meaning to your marriage relationship. For example, during foreplay or lovemaking when a couple engages in caressing, fondling, cuddling, kissing and touching each other's bodies and sexual organs. There is a 100% possibility of knowing through facial expressions, gestures, body movement, posture and physical distance whether one is faking or genuinely enjoying the act. In fact, through nonverbal communication the couple is kept informed throughout the whole duration of lovemaking and able to adjust accordingly.

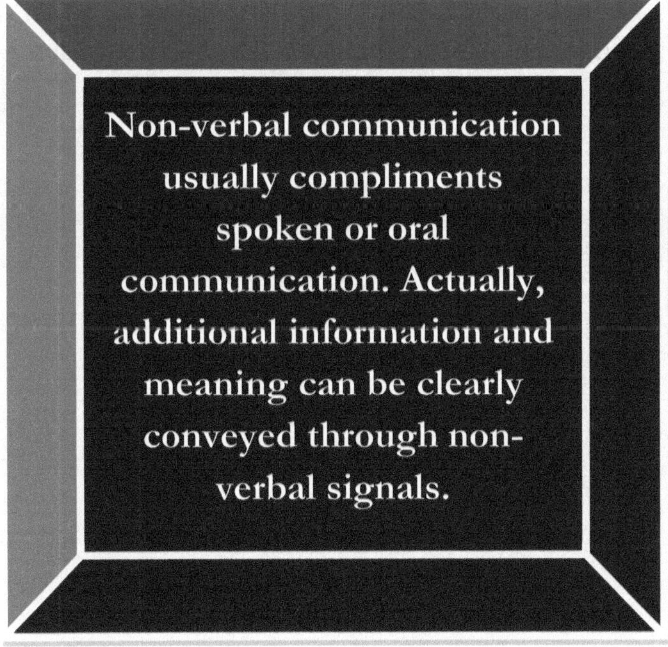

BARRIERS TO EFFECTIVE LISTENING

Noise in any form especially physical noise can be a hindrance to effective listening.

- **Lack of interest** - If you do not have interest in what is being discussed; you may not pay particular attention.

- **Being pre-occupied** with what to say next to the point of stopping listening to your spouse.

- **If the discussion is too long** - i.e. prolonged conversation might bore the listener.

- **Use of jargon** - If the sender uses technical terms to a lay person, it might be difficult to understand.

- **Distrust** - Individuals who do not trust each other are not likely to listen to each other.

- **Prejudice** - Judging the speaker by his/her appearance or manner of speech may be a barrier to listening.

- **Overload** - Giving the listener too much information at any given point thereby confusing them.

- **Language differences** - If the language being used is strange to a spouse it can be a barrier to effective listening.

- **Hearing impairment** - If the listener has some hearing disabilities it can create problems in listening.

TIPS ON HOW A SPOUSE CAN DEVELOP EXCELLENT LISTENING SKILLS

The following are tips on how a spouse can develop excellent listening skills;

i)   Paying attention throughout the conversation .

ii)   Maintaining eye contact with the speaker.

iii)   Seeking clarifications where not clear.

iv)   Avoiding interruptions during a conversation.

v)   Does not prejudge the speaker Sit upright during a discussion.

vi)   Avoid inertia by being active during a conversation.

COMMUNICATION IS KEY IN A MARRIAGE RELATIONSHIP

Stop entertaining thoughts of divorcing your spouse based on petty or unjustifiable reasons of what you call irreconcilable differences or not being compatible. Swallow your pride, in humility you can easily work out your differences as a couple.

Usually, what makes a couple fail to agree is mostly due to selfishness, greedy and pride. **Selfishness** talks of caring about yourself rather than about your friend (Self-centredness). **Greedy** means wanting more power or dominance over your partner. **Pride** means a feeling that you are more important or better than your spouse. Be humble, if you truly love your spouse you will be willing to sacrifice for her/him. Stop blaming each other over issues that you can easily discuss and resolve amicably. Learn to forgive each other and let go of bitterness, anger/resentment. Calm down, be tolerant! Put yourself in your partner's shoes, love doesn't insist on its own way.

"Above all, love each other deeply, because love covers over a multitude of sins" **1 Peter 4:8**

Don't give the devil an inch of control in your marriage or else he will claim a mile. Protect your marriage by not getting advice from wrong people. If you seek marital advice get it from mature, sober and God fearing marriage counselors.

Marriage between husband and wife is a legally binding agreement which should not be entered into lightly. It is instituted by God, whether one is a Christian or not. Marriage is a lifetime commitment.

"So they are no longer two, but one. Therefore what God has joined together let man not separate." **Matthews 19:6**

"I hate divorce, says the Lord God of Israel." **Malachi 2:16**

When a divorce has been effected women and children are the most affected.

My advice to the newly married couple is that they need to exercise a lot of patience. Marriage is not as simple as many people think. It is riddled with many different challenges, and to solve them you will require a new mindset or software of advanced modern techniques and technologies of counseling powered by the Holy Ghost. The days are long gone of relaying on an old mindset or software of obsolete type of techniques and technologies. For instance nowadays both husband and wife need to be in gainful employment so as to have multiple streams of income in a home. Therefore, this will imply that both husband and wife will knock off from work almost at the same time. If you don't have a maid then it will mean that you will have no choice but do house chores yourselves. In olden days a married woman would be restricted only to the role of a house wife. However, things are different now.

52

CHAPTER THREE

THE POWER OF LOVE

THE POWER OF LOVE

The power of love is dynamic, it can even be explosive in a positive or negative sense. The Bible clearly states that,

"The love of money is a root of all kinds evil, for which some have gone astray from the faith in their greediness, and pierced themselves through with many sorrows". - (1 Timothy 6:10)

There are three most interesting talked about topics in the world today centered on the power of love namely; the love of Power, the love of money, and the love of Sex. These are popularly known as the three pleasures of the world today. In trying to have the pleasure of power, money and sex, many people have ruined their lives.

The an unending wars and rumours of wars in the world today is as a result of people trying to have or cling on to power at all cost.

In pursuit of the pleasures of money people tend to engage themselves in evil activities in order to accumulate wealth.

The other most interesting talked about and sought after topic in the world today is on the subject of sex. A day cannot pass without talking about sex. This craving for sex, has led some section of society to adopt extreme and barbaric sexual practices such as Chidyelano in the Eastern province of Zambia. This practice allows married men to have sexual relations with wives of other men within a community.

When the power of love is motivated by a good ideology it can glorify God and be a blessing to mankind, but when motivated by an evil ideology it can glorify the devil and be a curse to mankind. Actually, what led the NAZIS to commit acts of horror against the Jews by killing millions of them in the 1930s and 1940s through the holocaust in concentrated camps was an evil ideology. These people were blinded by their belief and love in an evil ideology. Their evil acts were motivated and driven by the power of love for this ideology.

When the power of love is motivated by a good ideology it can glorify God and be a blessing to mankind, but when motivated by an evil ideology it can glorify the devil and be a curse to mankind.

The apostle Paul was also blinded by an evil ideology. He was driven by the power of love for his evil ideology against Christians. He passionately persecuted and killed many Christians thinking that he was serving God and yet not.

"Then Saul, still breathing threats and murder against the disciples of the Lord, went to the high priest and asked letters from him to the synagogues of Damascus, so that if he found any who were of the way, whether men or women, he might bring them bound to Jerusalem." **Acts 9:1-2.**

If not well handled or controlled the power of love in an evil ideology can extremely be dangerous, suicidal and counterproductive to any society. Its main purpose is to wipe out any perceived threat or danger to its belief core system. Great destinies of many people: Presidents, kings, and celebrities have been ruined. They have become casualties of the power of misplaced love. In the bible we have examples of people who suffered and had their careers ruined because they could not positively handle the power of love. For example Adam and Eve, David and Berth Shaba, Samson and Delilah.

Adam was mesmerised by the beauty and companionship of his wife. Actually in the presence of his beautiful wife Eve, he could not discern or use common sense or discretion to question the decision/behavior and attitude of Eve his wife, when she was deceived by the devil to eat of the forbidden fruit. His love for Eve was so strong such that he was blinded by it and failed to resist the temptation when she gave him also of the forbidden fruit to eat.

When you are caught up in a love affair with someone either married or single, it is almost impossible to break up because of the power of love. One would ask, is it possible to fall in love with another person who is not your spouse. The answer is an emphatic yes, it is very much possible to fall in love with another person especially if you become careless and cross set boundaries. Any relationship ought to have boundaries which must be respected e.g. relationships such as father and daughter, mother and son, brother and sister, nephew and auntie, uncle and niece, and cousins. And brother and sister in the lord. We have heard stories in our communities were father had carnal knowledge of his own biological daughter and we wonder how. This is because somewhere somehow someone ignored and crossed the legal set relationship boundaries and ended up committing the sin of incest.

Even at work places relationship set boundaries ought to be respected between male/female senior management staff and male/female junior employees. In short we need to avoid the spirit of familiarity, because familiarity breeds contempt.

The common mistake most people make is to be overconfident or overrate themselves in terms of their capacity or grace to contain or overcome temptation. They think that even though they spend more time with a friend of the opposite sex in person, on phone, and on the internet/social media nothing sinister could happen to make them victims by compromising and fall in a trap. In most cases it just happens regardless of how strong someone is spiritually. Remember there is actually what is called love at first sight. They forget that each time spent together strengthens the bond of love and intimacy between them. Affairs don't just happen, but slowly and unintentional develop from one level of friendship into another and eventually into more intimate sexual relationship. They evolve from mere or ordinary friendship into special, and finally graduate to sexual partners or lovers.

Ordinary Friends: These are merely good friends, where occasionally they greet each other, but don't matter much. They are casual relationships, no strings attached and emotionally not attached to each other in an intimate manner.

Special Friends: These are best friends and share a lot of things in common. They are emotionally attached to each other. It is in this category where as best friends you confide in each other, and sympathize with each other. In short they know each other's strengths and weaknesses.

Lovers: Usually it involves a partner in a romantic or sexual relationship or someone with whom a married person is having a love affair with. This is a deep, more passionate, and involves full blown intimate sexual relations.

One preacher said, when he is driving or walking with his wife and sees a beautiful woman, the rule is to look at her once and continue with the journey while praising God. Don't make a mistake of looking at a woman lustfully and spend more time admiring her.

Infidelity or adulterous affairs don't just happen, but usually begin with inappropriate friendships. Therefore protect your marriage by avoiding unnecessary friendships of the opposite sex, and terminating all private communications and intimate conversations with them. Let your spouse be your best friend and confidant.

"What God has joined together, let no one separate." **Matthew 19:5**

Joseph in the bible is a good example of someone who resisted this temptation successfully by literally fleeing from the wife of Potiphar. He refused to be entertained by the lustful advances of Potiphar's wife. She tried very hard to entice him, but failed lamentably. Her wicked schemes could not work.

Don't awaken or arouse love in a wrong way. After king David saw the beautiful Bathsheba bathing from the palace roof, he entered into an adulterous affair with her which had tragic consequences for his family and Israel.

"One evening David got up from his bed and walked around on the roof of the palace. From the roof he saw a woman bathing. The woman was very beautiful, and David sent someone to find out about her. The man said, "She is Bathsheba, the daughter of Eliam and the wife of Uriah the Hittite." Then David sent messengers to get her. She came to him, and he slept with her." **2 Samuel 11:2-4 NIV**

"Daughters of Jerusalem, I charge you: Do not arouse or awaken love until it so desires." **Song of Solomon 8:4**

Samson loved Delilah very much such that he was enticed and compelled to reveal the secret of his strength to her after she was bribed by the lords of philistines to discover the source of his strength. She actually ordered a servant to cut Samson's hair while he was sleeping, and then betrayed him to his enemies the Philistines.

"And it came to pass afterward, that he loved a woman in the valley of Sorek, whose name was Delilah" **Judges 16:4**

However, on the contrary our Lord Jesus Christ was motivated by the power of love positively. He sacrificed himself for the church so that he could present it to himself a glorious church, not having spot, or wrinkle, or any such thing; but that it should be holy and without blemish. Our lord Jesus Christ knowing fully well about the power of love, He decided to exhort husbands to love their wives as themselves.

The actualization of the celebration of true Love and Sexual fulfillment in marriage as God originally intended, is anchored on the premise of the power of love between husband and wife. True love and intimacy in marriage is a depiction of the love relationship between Christ (bridegroom) and the church (bride).

The husband is implored to love his wife as Christ also loved the church. The love and intimate sexual union between a husband and wife is a reflection of the true love, oneness and intimacy that exists between Christ and the church. The church ought to reverence Christ and give him all the praise and worship due unto him. In the same manner wives are implored to give reverence unto their husbands. The marriage relationship is the only relationship in which one can literally adore a spouse. It is the only relationship where a couple experience one fresh principle through intimacy and sexual union.

It is a relationship where the husband occupies the office of headship over the wife as Christ does for the church. It is a relationship where the wife is subject unto the husband in everything as the church is to Christ. It is a relationship where the husband sacrificially ought to love the wife as Christ loved the church and sacrificed himself for it.

The main reason Christ sacrificed himself was as follows:

a) To sanctify and cleanse the church with the washing of the water by the word

b) To present it to himself a glorious church, not having spot, or wrinkle, or any such thing; but that it should be holy and without blemish.

Our lord Jesus Christ was motivated by the power of love for the church, hence sacrificed his life by dying on the cross of Calvary in order to redeem the church from the power of sin.

Therefore, we as husbands ought to be motivated by the power of love for our wives by sacrificing ourselves for their wellbeing. We ought to love our wives with every fibre of our being. In everything we do or think let love lead.

'For the husband is the head of the wife, even as Christ is the head of the church: and he is the Saviour of the body. Therefore as the church is subject unto Christ, so let the wives be to their own husbands in everything. Husbands, love your wives, even as Christ also loved the church, and gave himself for it; that he might sanctify and cleanse it with the washing of the water by the word, that he might present it to himself a glorious church, not having spot, or wrinkle, or any such thing; but that it should be holy and without blemish. So ought men to

love their wives as their own bodies. He that loveth his wife loveth himself. For no man ever yet hated his own flesh; but nourisheth and cherisheth it, even as the Lord the church: For we are members of his body, of his flesh, and of his bones. For this cause shall a man leave his father and mother, and shall be joined unto his wife, and they two shall be one flesh. This is a great mystery: but I speak concerning Christ and the church. Nevertheless let every one of you in particular so love his wife even as himself; and the wife see that she reverence her husband." **Ephesians 5:23-33**

"Marriage should be honoured by all, And the marriage bed kept pure, for God will judge the adulterer and all the sexually immoral." **Hebrew 13:4 (NIV).**

There was something I got fed-up with; Hollywood teaching us about sex. They have managed to make sex look dark and dirty, and yet God created our male organs and female organs to enable us to express ourselves sexually in the bounds of marriage. Yes sex is holy but outside marriage its dirty ,in marriage its holy. Just like a woman can respond to her husband sexually so do we respond to God in worship, worship is responding to God's love.

CHAPTER FOUR

THE PRINCIPLES OF A LOVING HUSBAND

*"Wisdom is the principal thing; therefore get wisdom. And in all your getting, get understanding." - **Proverbs 4:7***

PRINCIPLE 1: PROVIDING LEADERSHIP

A home is an institution with organizational leadership structure in place. Therefore, for any institution or organization to function normally and fulfill its mandate, it has to have a leadership structure in place. This is no difference with marriage. In the organizational leadership structure for a home, the husband is head and assisted by his wife as a suitable helpmate. (Ephesians 6:4, Deuteronomy 6:6-7). The husband must clearly share the vision of his marriage with his wife. The mission statement of the marriage needs to be well articulated. The shared goals of the marriage ought to be clearly explained to the wife and family.

Therefore, the first fundamental principle of a loving Husband is basically to provide leadership to his wife and family. Man was wired differently from a woman. Actually, both men and women have difficulties understanding each other even reasoning is different, but according to God's creation man is the head of the woman and as such he ought to lead with love. In fact, the husband should emulate the leadership style of our lord Jesus Christ. Even though he was a leader, yet He chose to wash his disciples' feet. What a great leader to emulate!

Husbands are implored to lead with understanding and love knowing that a woman is a weaker partner and should be treated with respect. If you fail to apply wisdom in the manner in which you live with your wife the whole house will be on fire. However, the first fundamental principle of a loving husband is to take full responsibility of his leadership role in marriage as God intended.

PRINCIPLE 2: LOVE YOUR WIFE UNCONDITIONALLY

It is the responsibility or role of every husband to love his wife regardless of her characteristic flaws. Actually, this calls for total humility and sacrifice on the part of the husband. Husbands ought to give unconditional love to their wives. This is the God kind of love which is unmerited. Meaning that there should be no preconditions whatsoever before expressing it. As a matter of fact don't expect anything in return, but just do it with joy knowing that you are fulfilling one of your most important responsibilities to her.

Therefore, the Oxford Advanced Learners Dictionary defines **Romantic Love** as; a strong feeling of affection for somebody that you are sexually attracted to. It is the emotional expression of total affection for somebody that you adore, treasure, cherish, reverence, sexually attracted to and hold in high esteem.

This love can be expressed in many different ways. Don't become naive of the fact that she is now your wife and become complacent, but consider it as an honour and privilege. Therefore do the needful to her. Every time you wake up remind yourself that the most important thing that has ever happened to you is marry your dear wife. Remember, that the first time you saw her you became attracted and captivated by her beauty- outward and true inner beauty. It's now your total responsibility to see to it that you enhance/ complement her beauty lavishly. It's imperative for every man to learn how to love, nature and cherish his wife as a companion. It's not easy to understand a woman or better still please her. Every man ought to ask for wisdom from God in order to discern and respond to his wife's needs knowledgeably. ***Ephesians 5:25***

A woman (wife) was created primarily to provide companionship to man (husband). Hence a wife ought to bring joy, happiness, pleasure, fulfillment and completeness to her husband. And this is true especially if you look at the way God structured a woman's body. God knew exactly how man would feel upon seeing his wife being presented to him. So irresistible, beautiful, tender, attractive and appealing to man. Therefore if a husband is to enjoy the full benefits of having a wife, he needs to learn to treat her right.

PRINCIPLE 3: SPEND QUALITY TIME WITH YOUR WIFE

Spending quality time with your wife is the most important, treasured and fulfilling moment to her. This time ought to be exclusively given to her because it fulfills one of her most important needs-Affection. Give her a hug and a kiss when you arrive at home...talk to her and listen attentively as she shares her thoughts of the day with you. This is an opportune time for a woman to pour out her heart to her husband. This is the right time to off load or share whatever issues and challenges she encountered in the course of the day. Treat her as your queen by spending quality time with her. If you are at home make sure that there are no distractions. Switch off your phones, radio, television set and see to it that you don't read a newspaper, a book or allow children to make noise and run around in your home while talking to her. All she needs at this moment is your full undivided attention.

"....your desire will be for your husband, And he will rule over you".
Genesis 3:16

PRINCIPLE 4: RENDER ACTS OF SERVICE AND KINDNESS TO YOUR WIFE

When God first made man and put him in the garden of Eden. He gave him an assignment to tend and keep the garden. Therefore, any husband must always remember that all household chores in a home are his sole responsibility. The wife is merely a suitable helpmate and her role is to assist her husband tend and keep the home. However, in Zambia and most African countries our women folk have been subject to inhumane treatment by their husbands. Most often, three quarters of household chores are handled by wives. As a result they hardly find time to rest and enjoy marriage. Husbands should learn to render acts of service and kindness to their wives by doing house chores. A loving husband should always be of service to his wife by cleaning the dishes, washing, cooking, sweeping, gardening, bathing and taking care of the children, preparing the bed, and doing the laundry.

These include specifically providing some senseless acts of kindness and love to your wife, such as serving her early in the morning while she is still in bed or when back from work by making a warm cup of tea/coffee, or some cold juice. After work, make sure to call her on the way home so that she knows when to expect you.

When you are with your wife pay attention to her and be a man full of discernment; bring her flowers once in a while as a surprise. Buy a card often and write honestly of your appreciation and love for her. Buy her gifts for all special occasions such as on her birthday, Wedding Anniversary and etc. Take her out for a date night. Love should be in the air; be quick to open the car door when she wants to board or disembark a car. Time and again buy her gifts or presents. Women love to receive gifts of all kinds.

> **When you are with your wife pay attention to her and be a man full of discernment.**

PRINCIPLE 5: GIVE PHYSICAL INTIMACY TO YOUR WIFE

Physical intimacy is a very important component in a loving marriage relationship. For instance, the moment a baby is born cries for the attention of its mother. The crying of a little baby implies that it needs the mother's attention, affection and care. However, the baby stops crying immediately the mother or father embraces it. Usually, when the mother embraces the baby and allows it to breastfeed. There is an emotional and physical bond created. This is therefore, a sign that a newly born baby enjoys and yearns for physical intimacy with the mother or the father.

Similarly, often times the wife yearns for affection from the husband. Therefore, hug and kiss your wife every morning while you are still in bed. Kiss and embrace her before you leave for work. Hold her hand tightly as you take a walk. Hug and kiss her every night before you go to sleep. Physical intimacy is very important in a marriage relationship. It is a very powerful medium of non-verbal communication. Through it you can offer comfort and encouragement during low moments in the life of your wife. During moments of joy and happiness you can offer or convey sincere heartfelt congratulatory messages and solidarity to your wife as you embrace and hug her.

Physical touch can also be used to give your wife a sensational therapeutical massage to relieve her of stress. Give her a soothing body massage. Even when you are taking a walk in the park or along the beach you can hold hands as lovers signifying oneness as companions.

PRINCIPLE 6: PRAISE YOUR WIFE VERBALLY

When your wife is looking beautiful compliment her instead of just keeping quiet. This is a big mistake, a woman always loves it when she hears words of affirmation verbalized by her own husband. So when you see your wife looking beautiful don't hesitate to appreciate or shower her with praises. It is your duty to compliment your wife. Therefore don't wait until she hears some nice words of appreciation from another man. Tell her that you love her while you are in bed or having breakfast. Your wife takes delight in receiving words of affirmation. Call her during the day to see how she is doing and also send her some love text messages about how much you miss her. The husband telling the wife verbally some sweet and edifying words of affirmation such as;

'You are the most beautiful woman in the whole world.' 'You are a breath of fresh air to my life.' 'I can't live without you.'

You can actually post words of affirmation on the timeline of your wife on social media. When you make this announcement publicly it will definitely please and bring so much joy to her. Remember to post some nice and encouraging words on her timeline on the occasion of her birthday or marriage anniversary. This gesture of love will bring forth fresh memories of her past experiences. It will evoke precious memories of love and marital bliss.

Always remember to appreciate & acknowledge your wife.

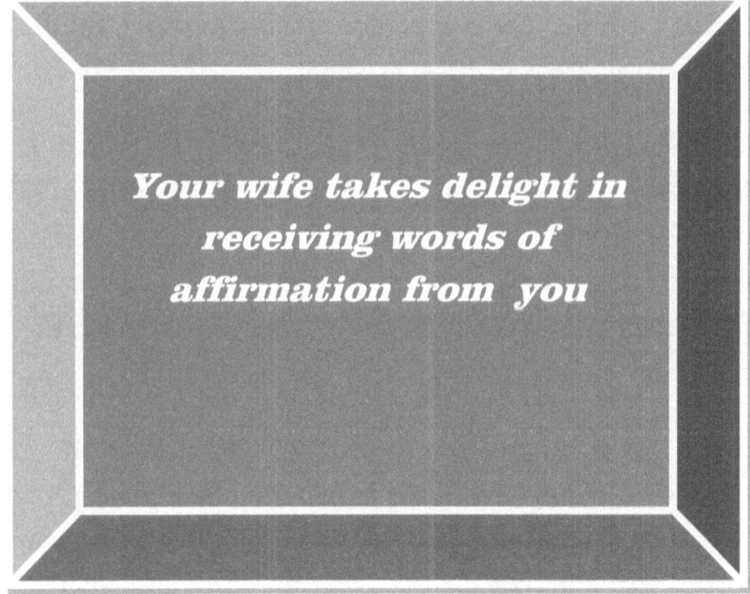

PRINCIPLE 7: TREAT YOUR WIFE WITH RESPECT

Treat your wife with respect, dignity and honour. Cherish your woman and make her feel loved. She is not a slave, but suitable help mate to you. Nowadays, most of married women are actually desperate for love. It seems that they are being deprived of the much needed or sought after warmth of love in their marriages, hence the desperation for this important yet unmet need. This desperation is very dangerous if left unchecked and unattended to for a long period of time. The temptation of looking for a romantic lover elsewhere is usually very high.

These desperate house wives could easily fall prey to men who seem to be charming, entertaining and promise to offer love and affection. The status of such men in question is immaterial. However, this behaviour or conduct undermines the very foundation, security and integrity of marriage.

Some wives do not receive enough affection from their husbands to meet their emotional love requirement. A wife whose emotional love requirement is met is a stable, happy, joyous, productive, focused, fruitful and fulfilled person. She is like a tree planted by the streams of waters, ever green, bearing healthy fruit throughout her life. She is an asset to her husband. In fact, it's the desire and dream of every woman to have this need for affection met by her husband.

The intelligence of our women folk is unmatched. It is almost impossible to fool them. They can easily notice when the measure of love from their husbands has gone down. When a woman senses that she is not getting as much love as she should from her husband she automatically becomes suspicious. She will start suspecting the husband of having a love affair with some other woman.

However, women who do not believe in God (non-believers) go to extremes of even doing weird things with an intention to win back love from their husbands. There's a longing or craving in their hearts for true love. I'm sure most of us are familiar with the term love potion. This is commonly practiced by women who are bound by the devil and whose conscious is dead. These poor women do all sorts of wicked things at the instructions of witch doctors (Ng'anga, in my native tongue) with a belief to win back the love they mostly crave for from their husbands.

"Husbands, love your wives, just as Christ also loved the church and gave himself for her" **Ephesians 5:25.**

Remember, she is only a helper to you, so don't be abusive by overload her with all house chores, but instead give her a lot of affection. Give her an overdose of it. If you sow goodness in your wife, you will also reap goodness.

"Do not be deceived, God is not mocked: for whatever a man sows, that he will also reap." **Galatians 6:7**

PRINCIPLE 8: HANDLE YOUR WIFE WITH GREAT CARE

Women are basically fragile hence the need to handle them with great care. Women are different from men therefore live knowledgeably with them. When you don't know the purpose of a thing abuse is inevitable. The Bible in the book of **Hosea 4:6,** says that, "my people perish for lack of knowledge."

And the bible in the book of **Proverbs 18:22,** says that, *"He who find a wife finds a good thing and obtains favour from the Lord."*

We need to understand that women are different from men in many aspects of life. For instance, in terms of sexual arousal, a man can easily be aroused by the sight of a nude woman, but not so with a woman. A woman needs more time of preparation before she can get aroused. When a woman is penetrated by her husband before being prepared adequately is tantamount to rape. In my observation as a marriage counselor, I have noted with concern that women who have been raped before are usually left wounded, bruised, emotionally, mentally and physically. The ego of such women is completely crushed. It is really a traumatizing experience especially when you hear it from the victim herself. As she explains the rape ordeal you can literally see the pain and anguish in her face. After the ordeal she is left powerless, confused, in great pain, bitter and resentful, and feels worthless. The victim becomes wounded emotionally and usually, the scars of rape often take years to heal. In fact even married women go through such traumatizing experiences inflicted on them by their own husbands. This makes sad reading indeed that the perpetrators of this crime are husbands themselves who are supposed to protect these vulnerable women. The bible says that the marriage bed is holy and undefiled. We need to go back to the basics and bring back sanity to the marriage bed.

"Let each one of you love his wife as himself, And let the wife see that she respects her husband." **Ephesians 5:33**

A Word to Husbands

Husbands, likewise, dwell with them with understanding, giving honor to the wife, as to the weaker **(sensitive),** vessel and as being heirs together of the grace of life, that your prayers may not be hindered. **(1 Pet. 3:7. KJV) paraphrased.**

PRINCIPLE 9: PROVIDE FOR YOUR WIFE & FAMILY

The third major role of a husband in marriage is to provide for his wife and family. The husband is the official bread winner in marriage. His world revolves around work and the woman's world revolves around man. It is the sole responsibility of every man to work and provide food, shelter, financial resources and clothing for his wife and children. Any man who doesn't work must not eat.

2 Thessalonians 3:10, Ephesians 6:6-8

Men ought not to be lazy, but assume their headship role in marriage. Remember, the first responsibility given to man by God was tillage of the land. The primary role of man is to work in order to provide a livelihood for his wife and family.

"Because you have listened [attentively] to the voice of your wife, and have eaten [fruit] from the tree about which I commanded you, saying, 'You shall not eat of it'; The ground is [now] under a curse because of you; In sorrow and toil you shall eat [the fruit] of it All the days of your life." **Genesis 3:17-19 Amplified Bible (AMP)**

"He who cultivates his land will have Plenty of bread, But he who follows worthless people And frivolous pursuits will have plenty of poverty." **Proverbs 28:19, Amplified Bible (AMP)**

"If anyone fails to provide for his own, and especially for those of his own family, he has denied the faith (by disregarding its precepts) and is worse than an unbeliever (who fulfills his obligation in these matters)" **1 Timothy 5:8 Amplified Bible (AMP)**

PRINCIPLE 10: PROTECT YOUR WIFE

The fourth most important role of a husband in marriage is to provide protection - a covering over the wife. That is to protect/safeguard the peace and total wellbeing of a woman, spiritually, physically, emotionally and mentally.

Physically, women are considered to be weaker than men, even though some women could be bigger in stature than men, however their overall strength cannot be compared to that of men. Physically, she is not as strong as a man, yes the woman's body was built with the capacity, tenacity/endurance to handle child birth. Nevertheless, scientifically, it has been proven that a woman's body structure is stronger to bear pain than that of a man. During pregnancy, she is able to carry a baby in her womb for a period of nine months and able to contain birth pains at delivery. Despite being strong in this regard, her overall physical strength cannot match that of a man. Physically, men, though some might look small in stature are very strong and powerful compared to women, 1 Peter 3:7. This is why from time in memorial women have been looking up to men for protection from any form of danger or threat. And women tend to get tired more quickly than men. According to **Gary Smalley** in his book, **'The Joy of Committed Love', Men have been made physically stronger than women and a woman's blood contains more water and 20% fewer red blood cells. Since the**

red cells supply oxygen to the body, women tire more quickly than men.

On the average, men possess 50% more brute strength than women (40% of a man's body weight is muscle; 23% of a woman's).

Emotionally, women are not as strong as men. In difficulty times it's been very easy for women to express their emotions compared to men. Mostly, women are able to express their emotions easily while men use logical thinking to interpret particular situations. However, women mostly use intuitive thinking to understand every detail of a puzzle/picture. They tend to have a bigger picture of a prevailing circumstance. They involve emotions to interpret situations and can express their emotions through crying freely. Men have been programed or taught from childhood not to express their emotions through crying because of the fact that they are men. Crying is a sign of weakness and ought not to be associated with men. Spiritually, women are very vulnerable to temptations. It appears as if their spiritual antennas are dead/ not receptive to the voice of God. The fall of man in the Garden of Eden was precipitated by a woman called Eve. The wife to Job became a mouth piece for the devil. She tried to persuade her husband Job to sin against God.

She said, "Are you still maintaining your integrity? Curse God and die! **Job 2:9**

Therefore women need spiritual protection from the enemy the devil. First and foremost the husband should realise that he is a priest to his wife. Hence, the need for him to perform his priestly duties with diligence and the total seriousness it deserves. He ought to stand in the gap for his wife. He has to see to it that intercession, supplications and prayers are offered to God on her behalf. He should make sure that his wife is encouraged to attend bible study and prayer meetings at their local church.

The reason why Adam sinned in the garden of Eden was due to the fact that he had failed lamentably to provide a spiritual, physical and mental covering over his wife Eve. The question that one would want to ask is this, where was Adam when Eve was being tempted by the devil. Adam only showed up after the devil had convinced Eve to pluck and eat of the forbidden fruit. Without thinking Adam also partook and ate of the forbidden fruit which looked good for food, pleasing to the eye and desirable for wisdom.

This signifies the true nature of sin. Sin is always coated with sugar and very appealing to the eye. Most of the time the devil disguises himself as an angel of light. The devil took advantage of Adam's absence and started a conversation with Eve which sowed seeds of doubt and unbelief in her heart. As long as Eve was by her husband's side she was safe, but the moment she drifted away she became a target of the tempter-the devil. (Hebrews 10:25)

The Husband must always get involved and develop an interest in the day to day affairs of his wife. Get to know her hobbies. If she likes singing he should make sure to support or accompany her when it's time for her rehearsals. It should be in your interest to know who her friends are; be it at home in the neighborhood, church, school or work. Don't wait until it's too late to redeem a situation. Our women folk are usually the likely target of the devil and he allows them to be isolated or wonder away from the husband before launching an attack on them. Remember, you are a companion to your wife, hence develop an interest in her, you are a shareholder in her life therefore take an interest of what goes on in her life. Every shareholder in any viable business ought to have an interest in the day to day running of the business so that at the end of each financial year the company can declare its profits and give some huge dividends to the shareholders.

The lesson learnt from this incident is that we as men should never allow our wives to assume the headship role in marriage. All along Adam was in control until Eve appeared on the scene. Therefore, men should assume the role of headship in marriage as soon as they marry. The husband needs to protect his wife from his immediate relatives e.g.

her In-laws like father and mother, brothers and sisters. At times relatives can be a thorn in the flesh to the wife especially her mother in law, and brothers and sisters to the husband. Most of the time they would want to despise and undermine the authority of the wife in her own home. They tend to boast and take matters into their own hands and disregard the rules of that particular home. Usually, a woman is intimidated and ridiculed. They make life very difficult and unbearable for her in her own home.

A REAL MAN

1.) Doesn't beat up a woman.

2.) Doesn't look down upon a woman.

3.) Doesn't disrespect a woman.

4.) Doesn't overload her with house chores.

5.) Doesn't treat her as a slave.

6.) Doesn't use her as a sex object.

7.) Doesn't insult his woman.

8.) Doesn't deprive his woman sexually

9.) Doesn't cheat on her

10.) Doesn't let down his woman

But A REAL MAN always;

1.) Protects his woman.

2.) Provides for his woman.

3.) Helps his woman with house chores.

4.) Treats his woman with respect.

5.) Listens to his woman emphatically.

6.) Comforts his hurting woman.

7.) Prays for his woman.

8.) Helps his woman financially.

9.) Gives romance and affection to his woman.

10.) Loves his woman unconditionally.

"Likewise, husbands, live with your wives in an understanding way, showing honor to the woman as the weaker vessel, since they are heirs with you of the grace of life, so that your prayers may not be hindered." -
1Peter3:7

> **However, the first fundamental principle of a loving husband is to take full responsibility of his leadership role in marriage as God intended it to be.**

When it comes to providing leadership in a home husbands must always be sober minded, loving, understanding and showing great restraint especially when provoked or challenged by a woman. Quick to listen and slow to anger.

CHAPTER FIVE

THE PRINCIPLES OF
A VIRTUOUS WIFE

"Who can find a virtuous wife? For her worth is far above rubies. The heart of her husband safely trusts her; so he will have no lack of gain. She does him good and not evil all the days of her life." **Proverbs 31:10-12**

A principle is a moral rule or strong belief that influences your actions. Therefore, if the wife is to be successful in marriage she has to basically work on developing her character or inner true beauty. Generally speaking, women should aim at cultivating their inner true beauty to efficiently and effectively carry out their roles in marriage.

A godly woman's inner true beauty is priceless. In fact, this talks about the priceless virtue of an inner soul of a woman adorned with excellent characteristics; such as having a sweet and quiet spirit, generous heart, kind, submissive, considerate, a good listener, diligent, honesty, caring, loving, and being hospitable. Actually, when you take time to be in the company or presence of such a magnificent woman, you become captivated by her conduct as it reveals or reflects her true Inner beauty.

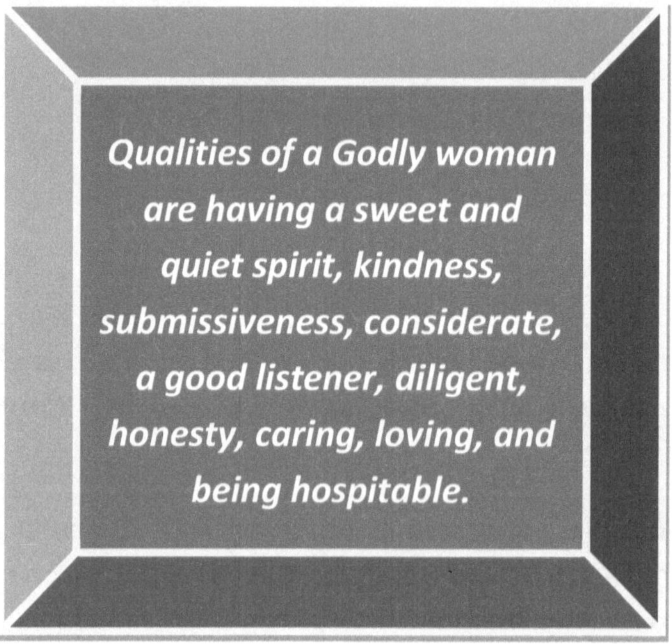

However, most of our women folk have actually treasured outward beauty at the expense of their inner true beauty. I strongly feel that there is need for women to concentrate more on beautifying their inner soul than on their outward appearance. The woman's inner beauty is of critical importance in fostering peace and harmony in our troubled marriages today, where advocacy for gender equality has become a norm. In fact there should be no room for competition between husband and wife in a home.

It doesn't matter how rich or highly educated a woman is, her fulfillment is in being submissive to her husband. A Godly woman possessing such an inner precious virtue would makes it easy for a lost and disillusioned man to come back to his senses, and then healing, reconciliation, salvation, and restoration of a broken marriage will become a reality.

"Wives, in the same way submit yourselves to your own husbands so that, if any of them do not believe the word, they may be won over without words by the behaviour of their wives, when they see the purity and reverence of your lives. Your beauty should not come from outward adornment, such as elaborate hairstyles and wearing of gold jewelry or fine clothes. Rather, it should be that of your inner self, the unfading beauty of a gentle and quiet spirit, which is of great worth in God's sight." **1 Peter 3:1-4**

PRINCIPLE 1: PROVIDE COMPANIONSHIP TO YOUR HUSBAND

A virtuous wife is always a companion to her husband. The wife's first core purpose is to provide companionship to her husband. This is indeed the woman's primary reason of creation. She was created from a man's rib. Which means that she should be there for her hubby at all times as an associate or suitable helpmate. In difficult times she ought to be by his side providing a shoulder to lean on, giving him the support, encouragement and comfort he deserves. When God first created man He said it is not good for man to be alone. Therefore the creation of a woman as a companion to man was not by coincidence, but by God's perfect design.

PRINCIPLE 2: SUBMIT TO YOUR HUSBAND

A virtuous wife is always submissive to her husband. Total submissiveness by the wife to the husband is a fundamental principle in marriage. The lion's greatest need is to be respected by the lioness. The Husband can be likened to a lion in charge of a pride. The alpha male lion is regarded as king in the lion kingdom - as head of the pride (a group of lions). In this kingdom there are principles that govern the behaviour of a pride - a lioness and cubs inclusive towards the lion king in-charge of a territory in a jungle or game reserve. Usually, when an animal has been killed by a pride, there is an order or protocol which is followed when the lions feed on their kill. The alpha male lion is entitled to feed first then the lioness. Lastly, the cubs are permitted to feed of the leftovers. The lioness and the cubs surrender the kill by laying down before the king as a sign of total submissiveness to his headship. When the lioness or cubs disobey protocol by tempting to feed first the consequences can be deadly. Therefore, the lioness and cubs are obliged to submit to the lion king in total humility and surrender. It is in fact mandatory that this principle of submissiveness is observed.

Source: http://africageographic.com

PRINCIPLE 3: RESPECT YOUR HUSBAND

"Let each one of you love his wife as himself, And let the wife see that she respects her husband." **Ephesians 5:33**

In fact, the husband's greatest need is to be respected, and the person he desires that respect from the most is his wife. He should not only deserve the wife's respect when he earns it. When respect is given even though he doesn't deserve it, it will motivate him to earn it. Domestic violence or wife battering can be avoided if women learned to respect their own husbands. One of the reasons why this evil is perpetrated is usually as a result of lack of respect for the husband by the wife. Please note, I'm not saying that wife battering should be condoned, but instead it should be condemned by every well-meaning citizen. However, don't take your husband for granted. Yes, he can be your best friend, but that doesn't permit you to lose respect for him. He deserves respect. Hold him in high esteem.

A virtuous wife always respects her husband: Respect is one of the most important virtues of a Godly wife. Learn to respect your husband for who he is and not for what he does. A woman must always respect her husband. Respect by the wife entails polite behaviour or care for her husband. She ought to do this in reverence to him as king and covering over her life.

A virtuous wife is never too busy for her husband because he is the reason for her creation. She makes sure that she is always available for him. She never allows him to be lonely again. She is a companionship to him for life. He needs her companionship and attention very much, therefore the wife should never be too busy for him. The wife should always endeavor to make his life comfortable. She should always serve and prepare him the food that he likes the most. Whenever he is dressing up she should be available to offer him guidance on the choice of attire.

A virtuous wife is always patient with her husband who is not perfect yet. So don't laugh at his mistakes or faults. Man is an enterprising being. He enjoys adventure. So as a wife be supportive to him in whatever field he chooses to explore as long as that field glorifies God. By doing so he is likely to make a lot of mistakes hence don't laugh at him, but be supportive and inspirational.

A virtuous wife doesn't make her husband feel replaceable, but cherishes him. She never lets him feel replaceable. Don't be in the company of certain women who disrespect their husbands. Regardless of his social status in life, he still deserves your respect. He is your king.

A virtuous wife never belittles her husband: Your husband is the king treat him with respect befitting a king. **You ought not to ridicule or belittle your husband** by making him seem unimportant to you in private or public life. In fact, the moment you ridicule or belittle your husband through verbal or non- verbal actions you are literally killing or destroying the very thing that in the first place attracted you to him, his ego or self-worth. By crushing his ego you are declaring a death sentence to his manhood. Manhood means the qualities that a man possesses, for example courage, strength, and sexual power.

Some women usually have a tendency of insulting their husband with impunity. They use unprintable words to tear their men down especially when the man fails to live by her expectations. Remember, your husband is the head and king over you, therefore always speak well of him. Don't talk to him as though he is a worthless person, but hold him in high esteem regardless of his inadequacies. But always remember that your husband deserves some respect. No matter how annoyed you are never insult or belittle your husband because the words spoken in anger can never be reversed.

A virtuous wife never talks to her husband on top of her voice, with an intention to silence him, but with tolerance endeavor to be an emphatic listener and ready to accommodate his opinion. If it is to criticize do it with love and respect. Never yell at him because that is being disrespectful.

A virtuous wife doesn't compare her husband with any man: She never puts any man before him. Man, like God is a jealous being and can't withstand the thought of another man competing for the attention of his wife. No wonder God does not allow any of His children to worship idols or any other created thing. God desires that all our attention is only directed to Him alone. In the same vein as a woman don't direct your attention to any man, but carefully give it all to your husband because he takes pride and delight in your company.

A virtuous wife doesn't boss her husband around, but with meekness she humbly submits to him. Therefore it is being disrespectful to boss him around. Meaning it is not in order for a wife to rudely give orders to her husband. Mind you he is your husband and so never look down on him.

A virtuous wife doesn't cause her husband to feel embarrassed, but tries by all means to cover his nakedness. Treat your husband with respect, honour, wisdom and dignity. He is your lord and king. Your duty as a wife is to protect your husband. When he makes a mistake cover him. If you were in the habit of sharing his weaknesses to your friends stop it. Don't undress your husband in public or before your friends. Never cause him to feel embarrassed. Remember you are his confidant and cheerleader.

A virtuous wife is always peaceable to her husband. When your husband is quiet, it doesn't necessarily mean that he is upset with you. Usually men once in a while enjoy having some quiet time alone either in meditation or reflection. They mostly use this quiet time to either meditate on the word of God or plan for the day ahead. Some men would enjoy spending some quiet time alone in the mornings while others in the evenings. It is during this quiet time that they replenish themselves for the task ahead. Our lord Jesus Christ used to spend some quiet time alone in prayer in the early hours of some mornings.

A virtuous wife is never possessive of her husband. A possessive wife doesn't want to share her husband with anyone else. As a result, this attitude always keeps her in bondage. She is always suspicious of her husband. She is often held captive by her own thoughts –the fear of losing her husband to other women, but a virtuous wife always trust her husband.

PRINCIPLE 4: AFFIRM YOUR HUSBAND

A virtuous wife always affirms & appreciates her husband. Every man takes pride in being a man by meeting all the basic and important needs of his wife sexually, emotionally, spiritually, physically, mentally, and materially etc. Usually by supporting or providing for his wife / family the husband feels contented as a man. Therefore, the moment a woman appreciates and shows gratitude to her beloved husband, the more the husband will be encouraged to even do greater exploits. Even when your husband fails to meet your basic needs, be an encouragement to him, don't look down upon him, but speak well of him. This will motivate him to work extra hard in order to meet your basic needs satisfactorily. As a wife acknowledge and affirm your husband verbally for always being kind and supportive to you. Shower him with some encouraging and edifying words of affirmation.

PRINCIPLE 5: MEET YOUR HUSBAND'S SEXUAL NEED

A virtuous wife always meets her husband's sexual need with joy. Meeting your husband's sexual need is an obligation which must be done with great joy and love. You should always see to it that you satisfy him sexually whenever you have an opportunity. Take delight in providing satisfactory conjugal services to him. A godly wife ought to offer her conjugal duties/services to her husband with joy and delight.

PRINCIPLE 6: BE A GOOD LISTENER TO YOUR HUSBAND

Empathy is the ability to understand and share the feelings of another. Therefore, a virtuous wife always gives her husband full attention. Never look away or texting while he is talking. By looking away or texting while he is talking you are literately saying i don't care about you and you are not important to me.

PRINCIPLE 7: MAKE YOUR HUSBAND FIRST PRIORITY

A virtuous wife always takes delight in her husband. Don't play down your need for him. Don't allow pride to control you and send a wrong signal to your husband pretending and behaving as though you don't need him and that you can do without him. The word of God says of a woman that her desire shall be for her husband. **Genesis3:16.**

PRINCIPLE 8: BE HONEST TO YOUR HUSBAND

A virtuous wife never manipulates her husband. He is your husband therefore don't take his love for you for granted. However, don't use his love for you and strong desire for sex as a bait or snare to manipulate him.

PRINCIPLE 9: BE CARING TO YOUR HUSBAND

She doesn't ignore her husband. She gives him an undivided attention. If given an opportunity to choose who to ignore between her husband and a female friend, she would rather ignore her friend than her husband. She always gives her husband an undivided attention. In most cases it is easier for a wife to ignore her husband than a female friend.

However, a husband should always be number one on the list of the things that matter the most in a woman's life

PRINCIPLE 10: BE DILIGENT

A virtuous wife is diligent in all that she does. Enterprising spirit is the mark of a virtuous wife. She is an industrious, creative (aesthetic) and a conscientious hardworking woman. She takes pleasure in working very hard in her home. When a man marries a woman he gives her a house and automatically she changes it into a beautiful home. The pride of every wife is in her home; the setting of her kitchen, dining room, living room and the bedroom matter a lot to her. A home is basically her main department therefore husbands will do better if they allow their wives to take full control of the overall outlook of a house; how to do the decoration, arrangement of house furniture, the type of her kitchen ware, combination of colours of her choice etc. All that she needs is a helping hand from her husband and a listening ear.

A REAL WOMAN

1.) Doesn't beat up her man

2.) Doesn't look down upon her man

3.) Doesn't disrespect her man

4.) Doesn't nag her man

5.) Doesn't deprive her man of sex

6.) Doesn't verbally abuse her man

7.) Doesn't misuse household income

8.) Doesn't gossip about her man

9.) Doesn't cheat on him

10.) Doesn't let down her man

But A REAL WOMAN always;

1.) Submits to her man

2.) Provides companionship to her man

3.) Helps his man with household chores

4.) Treats her man with respect

5.) Listens to her man emphatically

6.) Comforts her hurting man

7.) Prays for her man

8.) Helps his man lead the family

9.) Fulfills conjugal duties to her man

10.) Loves her man unconditionally.

Qualities of a Godly woman is having a sweet and quiet spirit, kindness, submissiveness, considerate, a good listener, diligent, honesty, caring, loving, and being hospitable.

CHAPTER SIX

UNDERSTANDING SEX IN
MARRIAGE

VAGINAL SEX: Is defined as sexual intercourse which basically involve the insertion and thrusting of the penis, when erect, into the vagina for sexual pleasure, reproduction, or both.

GREY AREAS OF SEX

I. **ORAL SEX:** Is defined basically as the insertion and thrusting of the penis, usually when erect, into the mouth or licking a vagina especially a clitoris, and penis for sexual pleasure. This practice is a conduit for Sexually transmitted diseases (STDs), if hygienic conditions are not observed.

II.   **MASTURBATION**: Is self-pleasuring or by fondling, caressing or touching, or stimulation of sexual organs to a point of release or ejaculation.

> *"My people are destroyed for lack of knowledge..." Hosea 4:6*

The practice of masturbation should be avoided at all cost. This is so because there is obviously a danger of becoming addicted to it. Once addicted to masturbation, sex with a woman becomes unenjoyably. And the victims' completely loose interest in normal sexual intercourse with a woman. The victims usually imagine that they are having sexual intercourse with someone during masturbation when in fact not. Men mainly have a problem in this area of masturbation and in as much as it may sound ironic in our culture some women too, have it and do masturbation as well. Medically speaking it may be looked at differently, but spiritually speaking it may led to bondage. There is an incident that was reported to us involving a married couple. The wife complained bitterly that her husband was in the habit of masturbating alone at night in their sitting room, in the pretext that he was watching television, when in the actual sense not. She couldn't understand the reason why her husband was fond of masturbation, when she was readily available to offer him vaginal sex.

Those who often practice masturbation are left with feelings of quilt and shame after the act itself. It is so embarrassing for one to engage in this vice when the spouse is readily available to help out.

SODOMY/HOMOSEXUALITY

HOMOSEXUALILITY: Is defined as a person, usually a man, who is sexually attracted to people of the same sex: sexual activity between two people of the same sex in which they touch each other's sexual organs, and which may include anal sex.

Biblically speaking, we all know that God never made Adam and Steve, but Adam and Eve, male and female, He created He them. *(Gen.1:27)*

SODOMY: According to the English Learners' dictionary, Sodomy is a sexual act in which a man puts his penis in somebody's, especially another man's anus.

SODOMY/ANAL SEX: Is defined basically as the insertion and thrusting of the penis, usually when erect, into the anus for sexual pleasure.

Anal sex is against the order of nature and is not a health practice. The main purpose of the anus is to excrete waste matters from the bowels. When the purpose of a thing is not known abuse is inevitable.

The name Sodomy is derived from the city of Sodom and Gomorrah which God destroyed because of the homosexuality that was going there.

GAY: Is defined as a man having unnatural sexual or physical activity with a fellow man, in which they touch each other's sexual organs, and which may include anal sex.

LESBIAN: Is defined as a woman having unnatural sexual or physical activity with a fellow woman, in which they touch each other's sexual organs.

"And they called to Lot and said to him, "Where are the men who came to you tonight? Bring them out to us that we may know them carnally" So Lot went out to them through the doorway, shut the door behind him. And said, "Please, my brethren, do not do so wickedly! **Genesis 19:5-7 NKJV.**

BESTIALITY: Is sexual activity between a human being and an animal. *(Exodus 22:19)*

INCEST: Is sexual activity between two people who are closely related in a family, for example, a brother and sister, a father and daughter, or mother and son. *(Leviticus 18:8-18)*

The Bible clearly states that;

"Whose minds the god of this age has blinded, who do not believe, lest the light of the gospel of the glory of Christ, who is the image of God, should shine on them." **2 Corinthians 4:4**

"For this reason God gave them up to vile passions. For even their women exchanged the natural use for what is against nature. Likewise also the men, leaving the natural use of the woman, burned in their lust for one another, men with men committing what is shameful, and receiving in themselves the penalty of their error which was due." **Romans 1:26-32**

THE PURPOSE OF VAGINAL SEX

Let us look at the purpose of vaginal sex in the context of marriage between a husband and wife. Basically, there are only two specific reasons for vaginal sex in marriage-reproduction and pleasure.

I.   REPRODUCTION/PROCREATION

Reproduction is the act or process of producing babies. Therefore, the primary purpose of sex is for procreation of the human race and for pleasure. Marriage between husband and wife was instituted by God in order to provide companionship and for procreation to ensure continuity of the human race.

II. PLEASURE

This is the excitement derived from the act of sex itself. It is a feeling of contentment and satisfaction that is experienced through the act of sex between husband and wife. God has wired us in such a way that both husband and wife have an inherent or in built desire for sexual pleasure.

SEX IN MARRIAGE

Sex is defined as a physical activity between two people a male and female in which they touch each other's sexual organs, and which may include sexual intercourse. Sexual intercourse is actually the insertion and thrusting of the penis which is a male sex organ, usually when erect, into the vagina which is a female sex organ for sexual pleasure, reproduction, or both. This is also known as vaginal intercourse/sex.

Remember sex ought to be practiced in the confines of marriage and not outside of it. Sex is very significant in the establishment of the institution of marriage and its existence. Without sex there is no consummation of marriage, without consummation of marriage, there is no union and without union the one flesh principle doesn't apply. Therefore without the application of the one flesh principle marriage is null and void.

One of the most important aspect of marriage is to provide a legal platform where a husband and wife can have their sexual needs meet within the confines of marriage. Hence marriage is the only institution where sex can be practiced legally. The husband is the only legally authorized person to render affection and conjugal obligations to his wife, and the wife is the only person legally authorized to render affection and conjugal obligations to her husband. In marriage both the husband and wife have a binding agreement which allows them to share their bodies to each other for sexual pleasure and reproduction. In other words they are permitted by law to offer their bodies to each other for intimacy and sexual pleasure, except with consent for a short period to devote themselves to prayer and fasting. As a matter of fact these are privileges and rights that husbands and wives ought to enjoy in marriage.

Let us look at the meaning of the word 'Defraud' in *1 Corinthians 7:5 in KJV Bible.*

According to the Merriam Webster Dictionary (https.//www.merriam-webster.com),defraud means to deprive of something by deception.

And the meaning of deception is the act of causing someone to accept as true or valid what is false or invalid.

The word deprive means to take (something) away from (someone or something): to not allow (someone or something) to have or keep (something).

Therefore, to defraud is when you actually intentionally deny or refuse your spouse access to your body for the sole purpose of meeting their sexual need. In other words, you choose to give unnecessary excuses in order to deprive your spouse of sex. Most often wives would use sickness as an excuse to deprive their husbands of sex. Don't deprive each other of sex, except by mutual consent over a short period of time so that you can devote yourselves to prayer and fasting or when one of you is not too well to engage in sexual activities.

In the last part *of 1 Corinthians Chapter 7 verse 5,* the apostle Paul observed with concern that married couples should not abstain from sexual intercourse for a longer period of time than necessary to avoid temptation.

He noted that it is possible for a sexually active married couple to fall into temptation of sexual immorality if denied an opportunity to have sex in a matrimonial home. In certain situation especially when a sexually active spouse is sexually aroused self-control can be outstripped due to lack of continence. So when faced with the temptation of committing sin of sexual immorality and you discover you are incontinency then the best option for you is to flee the scene without asking any questions. The Bible in the book of *Genesis 39:10-12,* clearly states that Potiphar's wife cast longing eyes on Joseph, and she tried to entice him to commit adultery with her, but failed because he ran away from the scene of temptation.

"So it was, as she spoke to Joseph day by day, that he did not heed her, to lie with her or to be with her. But it happened about this time, when Joseph went into the house to do his work, and none of the men of the house was inside, that she caught him by his garment, saying, "Lie with me." But he left his garment in her hand, and fled and ran outside." **Genesis 39:11-12**

"Flee sexual immorality. Every sin that a man does is outside the body, but he who commits sexual immorality sins against his own body. Or do you not know that your body is the temple of the Holy Spirit who is in you, whom you have from God, and you are not you own? For you were bought at a price; therefore glorify God in your body and in your spirit, which are God's." **1 Corinthians 6:18-20**

"Therefore let him who thinks he stands take heed lest he fall. No temptation has overtaken you except such as is common to man; but God is faithful, who will not allow you to be tempted beyond what you are able, but with the temptation will also make the way of escape, that you may be able to bear it." **1 Corinthians 10:12-13**

REASONS FOR A SEXLESS MARRIAGE

A sexless marriage is when a couple is having sex once or less in a month and less than ten times in a year. However, there is no guideline on how much sex is the right amount. Find below some reasons for a sexless marriage;

1.) **INFIDELITY:** It is the act of not being faithful to your spouse, by having sex with somebody else. Sexless marriage is the recipe for infidelity. A sexually deprived spouse is vulnerable to committing adultery. It is imperative to take preventive measures by ensuring that our partner is kept satisfied sexually at all times. It doesn't matter whether somebody is a pastor or not, but as long as their marital conjugal right is infringed they are bound to fall into the sin of adultery.

2.) **WORKAHOLIC:** A workaholic is a person who works very hard and finds it difficult to stop working and do other things. This attitude or love for work leaves him/her extremely exhausted to engage in meaningful sexual activities. If this person doesn't change and continues to bury his/her head in the sand sooner than later their marriage will be grappling with sexual deprivation.

3.) **RESENTMENT:** Is a feeling of anger or unhappiness about something that you think is unfair. So when you notice an emotional and physical withdraw from your spouse. It implies that your spouse is unhappy and this could be attributed to something that happened earlier on in the day. Therefore, ask yourself some questions. Maybe your wife is hurting because you didn't help her fix a leaking pipe. Maybe your husband is hurting because you didn't give him sex. Remember, resentment can build up over time and if you don't act fast to address the underlying issue you may end up shutting your spouse out emotionally.

So don't allow resentment to control you hence leave the communication lines open. When you notice a physical and emotional withdraw from your spouse don't get caught up in the same cobweb of resentment, but instead be bold enough to open up and talk about it. Do not expect your spouse to read your mind, guess or just know from without what you need or how you feel.

4.) **CRITICISM:** To positively criticize somebody is to say that you disapprove of something in a calm, loving, mature and helpful manner. This is called constructive criticism. Constructive criticism is meant to help somebody and not demonize them. However, negative criticism is meant to demonize and crush the ego of your spouse. Once you negatively criticize your husband his virility is completely crushed. If you negatively criticize your wife you are completely crushing her ego. You are literally making it very difficult for her to respond sexually.

5.) **COMPLAINTS:** To complain is to say that you are annoyed, unhappy or not satisfied about somebody or something. Complaints can be very devastating to your spouse. So be careful the way you express your grievances to your spouse. Furthermore, when you complain to your spouse you are basically expressing your ingratitude, frustration, and anger. You are literally saying that you are not being treated right. Frankly speaking, complaints can be a heavy load to carry. They weigh down the spirit of your spouse. They tend to immobilize the victim who is the recipient of complaints. Complaints can have adverse effects on the libido of the spouse. Therefore be mindful of the way you express your grievances to your spouse.

6.) **LOSS OF THE FIRST LOVE:** One's first experience of the feeling of romantic love. Your spouse was the first person to be the object of your romantic affection. There is usually a tendency to lose the first fires of passionate love when a couple gets old in marriage. Over the years the couple tend to take each other for granted. Where is the respect befitting your spouse? When you lose the first love for your spouse it becomes very difficult to engage in meaningful sexual relations. Sexual deprivation in quality and quantity becomes the norm. Rekindle the fires of passion of the first love.

"...It is good for a man not to touch a woman.

Nevertheless, to avoid fornication, let every man have his own wife, and let every woman have her own husband.

Let the husband render unto the wife due benevolence: and likewise also the wife unto the husband.

The wife hath not power of her own body, but the husband: and likewise also the husband hath not power of his own body, but the wife.

Defraud ye not one the other, except it be with consent for a time, that ye may give yourselves to fasting and prayer; and come together again, that Satan tempt you not for your incontinency."

1 Corinthians 7:1-5

"...It is good for a man not to touch a woman. Nevertheless, because of sexual immorality, let each man have his own wife, and let each woman have her own husband. Let the husband render to his wife the affection due her, and likewise also the wife to her husband. The wife does not have authority over her own body, but the husband does. And likewise the husband does not have authority over his own body, but the wife does. Do not deprive one another except with consent for a time that you may give yourselves to fasting and prayer; and come together again so that Satan does not tempt you because of your lack of self-control."

1 Corinthians 7:1-5 (NKJV)

114

CHAPTER SEVEN

THE MALE AND FEMALE SEXUAL ANATOMY

THE PARTS OF MALE EXTERNAL SEXUAL ANATOMY

The penis and scrotum are the two parts of the male external sex anatomy.

PENIS

The penis is made of three 3 layers of spongy tissue. When aroused sexually blood fills these tissues. The penis becomes hard and stands up, which is also called getting an erection or hard-on.

The average size of an adult erect penis is usually 5 to 7 inches long. The size of the penis when it is flaccid has got nothing to do with its size when it's hard. Often times some penises get bigger in size when they get hard, while others stay pretty much the same size.

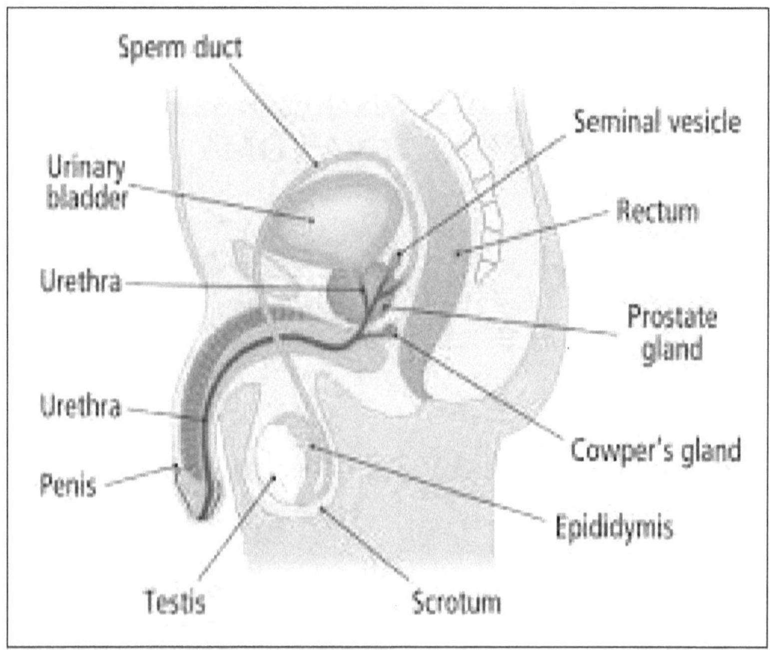

Figure 1: Male Sexual Anatomy

Every penis looks a little different. For instance, some curve like a banana when they are hard, while others are straighter, but all penises have the same parts though:

- **GLANS**

The glans is also called the head or tip of the penis. It has an opening of the urethra on its middle where pre-ejaculation of the secretions and semen come out of, and also the urine come out of this opening. This is actually the most sensitive part of the penis.

- ## SHAFT

The shaft of the penis extends from the tip to where it connects to the lower belly. It can be likened to a tube. In fact the urethra is inside the shaft.

- ## FORESKIN

The foreskin is a patch of skin that covers and protects the head (Glans).When the penis gets hard, the foreskin pulls back and the tip is exposed. Sometimes the foreskin is circumcised soon after birth or during adulthood.

- ## FRENULUM

The frenulum is where the foreskin meets the underside of the penis. Actually, it looks like a small V underneath the head of the penis, and usually part of it remains after circumcision. It is a very sensitive part.

- ## SCROTUM

The scrotum is the sac of skin that hangs below the penis. It is in this sac where the testicles are located and they are always kept at the right temperature. When it is too cold the scrotum pulls the testicles closer to the body, but when it is too warm, the testicles hang away from the body.

The scrotum is covered with wrinkly skin and hair. The scrotum can either be big or small. It can either have a little hair or a lot, and it also varies in colour. Some men have larger scrotums on one side than the other.

It is extremely sensitive and very painful when hit or twisted. It is pleasurable when touched gently during sex.

- **ANUS**

It is the opening to the rectum. The anus has lots of sensitive nerve endings and it is used to get rid of waste matters from the digestive system.

THE PARTS OF MALE INTERNAL SEXUAL ANATOMY

The internal parts of the male sex anatomy are made up of testicles, epididymis, vas deferens, seminal vesicles, prostate gland, Cowper's glands, urethra and cremaster.

- **TESTICLES**

The testicles are two ball-like glands inside the scrotum. They make sperms and hormones like testosterone.

- **EPIDIDYMIS**

The epididymis is a tube where the sperm matures. It connects each of the two testicles to each of the vas deferens. It also holds the sperm before ejaculation.

• VAS DEFERENS

A vas deferens is a long, narrow tube that carries sperm from the epididymis to the seminal vesicles during ejaculation. There are two of them connected to each epididymis.

• SEMINAL VESICLES

The seminal Vesicles are two small organs located below the bladder. They produce semen which is the fluid that sperm moves around in.

• PROSTATE GLAND

The prostate gland is the size of a walnut or golf ball and is located between the bladder and the penis. It is actually in front of the rectum. The prostate gland makes a fluid that protects and nourishes the sperm and helps it move. The prostate gland is sensitive to pressure or touch in a way that many people find pleasurable.

• COWPER'S GLANDS

The Cowper's gland produces a fluid called pre-ejaculate. This fluid prepares the urethra for ejaculation. It reduces friction so the semen can move more easily. The Cowper's glands are under the prostate and attach to the urethra. They are also called bulbourethral glands.

• URETHRA

The urethra is the tube that carries urine from the bladder to the outside of the body. When a man reaches orgasm semen is also ejaculated through the urethra. However, when the penis is erect during sex, the flow of urine is blocked from the urethra allowing only semen to be ejaculated out of the body.

• CREMASTER

It is a thin muscle consisting of loops of fibers derived from the internal oblique muscle and descending upon the spermatic cord to surround and suspend the testicle. Its main function is to control the temperature of the testicles. It can either lower or raise the testicles depending on the temperature in a particular environment. In other words, the cremaster is a muscle that moves the scrotum and testicles closer to the body when a man is cold, aroused and also when someone touches his inner thigh.

THE PARTS OF FEMALE EXTERNAL SEXUAL ANATOMY

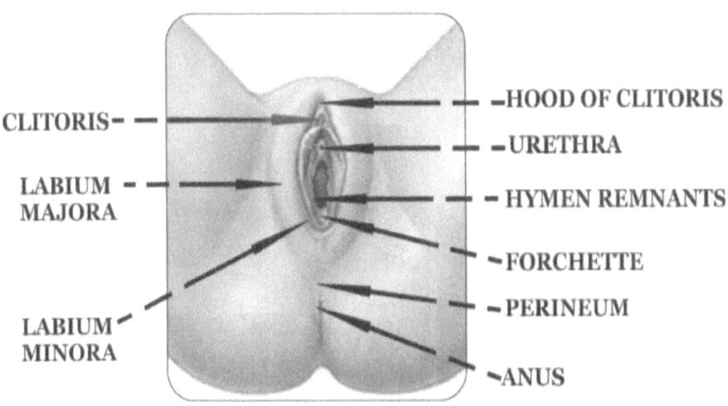

Figure 2: Female Sexual Anatomy

The vulva is the external part of the female genitals-Labia, clitoris, vaginal opening, and urethra.

- **LABIA**

These are lips which are folds of skin around the vaginal opening.

i)   **LABIA MAJORA:** These are outer lips and usually fleshy and covered with pubic hair.

ii)   **LABIA MINORA:** These are inner lips and are inside the outer lips. They extend from the tip of the clitoris to the lower part of the opening of the vagina. They usually vary in size and texture, some are short while others are long, wrinkled or smooth. Usually one lip is longer than the other. They also appear different in colour from pink to brownish black. As one gets older the colour of the labia changes as well. Many of the women folk have larger inner lips than the outer lips, and some have larger outer lips than inner lips. They are both sensitive, and swell when one is aroused.

• CLITORIS

The clitoris is located right at the top of the vulva, where the inner lips meet. The clitoris usually vary in size. Some can be like a pea while others are as big as a thumb. The clitoris has its tip covered by the clitoral hood.

The clitoris extends inside a woman's body on both sides of the vagina. The extension is called the shaft and its roots and legs called crura (refers to one of two tendinous structures that extends below the diaphragm to the vertebral column. There is a right crus and a left crus, which together form a tether for muscular contraction. They take their name from their leg-shaped appearance – crus meaning leg in Latin) .It is about 5 inches long.

The clitoris is made up of spongy tissue that becomes swollen when aroused. It has thousands of nerve endings more than any other part of the human body. **The only purpose of the clitoris is to make a woman feel good when aroused during lovemaking and sexual intercourse.**

- ## URETHRA

The urethral opening is located just below the clitoris and it is the tiny hole that is used to pee urine out of the bladder.

- ## VAGINA

The vaginal opening is located just below the urethral opening. This is the passage where menstrual blood leaves the body, and it is also where babies are born through.

- ## ANUS

The anus is the opening to the rectum. It has a lot of sensitive nerve endings. According to God's design its sole purpose is to excrete waste matters from the body. Therefore, it is morally very wrong for some people to use it for sexual pleasure.

- ## MONS PUBIS

The mons pubis is the fleshy mound above the vulva. Generally, after puberty pubic hair starts to grow around this area. Its main function is to cushion the pubic bone.

THE PARTS OF FEMALE INTERNAL SEXUAL ANATOMY

- **VAGINA**

The vagina is a tube connecting the vulva (outer part of the vagina) with the cervix and uterus (inner parts of the vagina).The vagina is really stretchy and expands when aroused.

- **CERVIX**

The cervix is located between the vagina and the uterus. It has an opening connecting the vagina and the uterus. It allows the menstrual blood out of the uterus, and also allows the sperm into the uterus. The cervix stretches open or dilates during childbirth.

One can actually feel the cervix when a penis or any other object is inserted into the vagina.

- **UTERUS**

The uterus is a muscular organ shaped like a pear and about the size of a small fist. It is often called the womb because it is where a fetus grows during pregnancy. Usually the lower part of the uterus lifts toward the belly button when sexually aroused. This is the reason why the vagina stretches or gets longer when aroused sexually.

- **FALLOPIAN TUBES**

These are two narrow tubes that carry eggs from the ovaries to the uterus. It is also a passage where sperm moves through to fertilize the egg.

- **FIMBRIAE**

The fimbriae look like tiny fingers at the end of each fallopian tube. When the ovary releases an egg, they help sweep it into the fallopian tube.

- **OVARIES**

The ovaries are used to store the eggs and they also produce hormones such as estrogen, progesterone, and testosterone. These hormones usually help to regulate menstrual cycles and pregnancy. It is during puberty that the ovaries start to release an egg each month until menopause. Sometimes more than one egg is released in a month.

- **BARTHOLIN'S GLANDS**

These are located near the vaginal opening. They often release fluid that lubricate the vagina when one is aroused sexually.

• SKENE'S GLANDS

The Skene's glands are located on either side of the urethral opening. They secrete or release fluid during female ejaculation. They are also called paraurethral glands or female prostate glands.

• HYMEN

The hymen is the thin fleshy tissue that covers or stretches across part of the opening to the vagina. Hymens differ a lot in how much of the vaginal opening they cover, and they can sometimes tear and cause bleeding the first few times you put something or an object in the vagina.

• G-SPOT

The G-Spot also popularly known as the Grafenberg spot is located on the front or belly-button side of the vagina. It is located a few inches on the inside of the vagina. The G-Spot usually swells when aroused sexually. It is one of the most sensitive sexual parts of the female human body. Most women feel excited when their G-Spot is stimulated by touch.

CHAPTER EIGHT

THE POWER OF
SEXUAL INTIMACY

SEXUAL INTIMACY

Sexual intimacy is the glue of marriage. It creates a strong bond between husband and wife. Actually, it is almost impossible to separate a couple in a marriage where sexual intimacy is practiced regularly. Whenever a couple meets to have sexual intimacy a hunger or yearning for more is created. This makes the couple to look forward for more of such times of sexual intimacy. They often become captivated by the presence of the significant other, as a result they tend to get obsessed with each other. To them nothing matters than to please their partner. The Bible says,

"But he who is married cares about the things of the world-how he may please his wife." **1 Corinthians 7:33 (NKJV)**

"…But she who is married cares about the things of the world-how she may please her husband." **1 Corinthians 7:34 (NKJV)**

In this world, married couples are ever preoccupied with the things that can help strengthen their marriage bond. As lovebirds, they both look for possible ways in which they can please each other. This longing for each other eventually culminates into sexual intimacy. Therefore, the desire or hunger for sexual intimacy is a necessity for a healthy and loving marriage relationship. Companionship between husband and wife will always put a demand on them to look forward for moments of refreshment through sexual intimacy. Sexual intimacy is the ultimate fulfillment which the couple derives in their marriage relationship. When it comes to having a fulfilling sexual encounter make sure to give it your best shot. You never undermine the power of sexual intimacy because it is the glue of marriage, therefore make it a habit to meet regularly as a couple and enjoy sex together so as to cement your relationship bond.

Sacrifice is a prerequisite to a satisfactory sexual encounter in marriage. Without sacrifice it is impossible to attain the ultimate sexual satisfaction. It will require the full sacrifice and cooperation of both the husband and wife to achieve a fulfilling sexual union. When you allow your egos to rule then both you and your wife will only concentrate at pleasing your own separate selfish desires. The Bible says, don't deprive each other sexually. Therefore, drop down all personal defenses and remain completely naked before your spouse. Offer your bodies as a living sacrifice. Remember, when you sacrifice for your spouse, his/her joy will become your joy. Actually it is quite fulfilling to see your hubby attain maximum sexual satisfaction. Find below some benefits of the power of sexual intimacy;

- Your risk of heart disease, stroke, and hypertension is reduced

- The blood pressure is controlled to normal

- It helps to strengthen muscles

- The overall condition of the heart health is improved

- It helps in burning calories

- Sex drive or libido is increased

- It improves Sleep

- It helps to reduce stress

THE ULTIMATE SEXUAL PLEASURE

Sex is one of the most important needs of man today. Either driven by its pleasure or the need for procreation of the human race, consciously or unconsciously we have been consumed by its whelms. Pursued by people of different age groups - both the old and young, whether married or unmarried.

It's the desire of almost every man and woman to pursue the pleasure of sex, unless one's hormones are disabled or not functional at all. Sex is a mystery, even children from a tender age tend to become aware of their sexuality, it appears that there is an inherent inborn/desire for sexual pleasure. At a tender age either moved by instinct or by some inbuilt /inborn sexual desire the child would be drawn sexually towards the opposite sex. However, it is very important to educate children about sex the moment they become aware of their sexuality. God in His infinite wisdom created man/woman with an inbuilt sexual software which can easily be activated from a tender age.

Sex is a gift and blessing from God. If well-handled it can be a source of great pleasure and harmony to married couples, but if not it can be a source of great pain, frustration, resentment and confusion.

Sex is a gift and blessing from God. If well-handled it can be a source of great pleasure and harmony to married couples, but if not it can be a source of great pain, frustration, resentment and confusion.

PREPARATION FOR SEXUAL
INTERCOURSE

So how does a couple prepare for an exciting and fulfilling sexual encounter?

1.) First and foremost the couple should always look forward to having a wonderful time of sexual intimacy.

They should both anticipate having a satisfying sexual encounter. Nothing happens by chance as I mentioned earlier in this book that to **every effect there is a cause.**

God has given us the power of imagination. In *Ephesians 3:20 (MSG)* *"God can do anything, you know-far more than you could ever imagine or guess or request in your wildest dreams! He does it not by pushing us around but by working within us, his Spirit deeply and gently within us."* Use your imaginations to paint a faith picture of what you want to experience in the natural realm. So in your imaginations see yourself with your spouse having an intriguing sexual experience. Unless a sexual experience is first birthed in your imaginations, it will be impossible to actualize it in the physical. It all starts in the mind. One has to be in the right frame of mind free from any disturbance or anxiety. The mind is a very powerful organ of the human body that has a bearing on sex. Capitalising on the use of all the five senses: Taste, Smell, Touch, Sight and Hearing/Sound to enhance your sexual experience can be a life changing experience to any couple desiring to achieve maximum sexual fulfillment. Therefore, sex basically starts by engaging and stimulating the mind through the five senses. The mind actually can be stimulated in the following ways in order to develop/build up interest/desire in sex in a more profound way.

Taste: The sense of taste is critical to stimulating your lover sexually. Therefore ensure to use to your advantage the sexual taste bud in order to enjoy to the maximum the delicious food of sex. You can as well use chocolate and other stimulants to enhance the sense of sexual taste during your lovemaking and sex experience.

Smell: The sense of smell is important in stimulating sexual feelings and enhance pleasure before, during and after sexual intercourse. Couples should always ensure to take a bath before and after sex. In fact male animals such as dogs mostly use the sense of smell to detect when the female is on heat. Actually, it is also possible for a husband to detect through the sense of smell that the wife is on heat and ready for sexual intercourse. Prepare your bedroom in advance by spraying nice perfumes to make your sex experience with your lover memorable.

Touch: You can as well make use of the sense of touch during lovemaking. Touch each other simultaneously in erotic areas of your body to stimulate sexual feelings. The sense of touch is critical to stimulating or arousing sexual desire. Therefore, embrace, caress, fondle, kiss each other as you explore and enjoy new discoveries of an unchartered territories of your lover's sexy body.

Sight: The sense of sight is critical in stimulating sexual feelings. Ensure to switch on the light in order to have the full view of your lovers well shaped and curved enticing body. Especially men are easily aroused by sight. Wives should learn to avoid getting into bed with the same clothes they wore the previous day. Make it a habit by wearing sexy see-through gown or night dress in order to entice your partner.

Hearing: The sense of hearing is also important to enhance your sexual experience with your lover. Hence be alert as you talk to each other during your lovemaking and sexual experience. As you employ the sense of hearing some intense groaning and crying sounds can be heard from your lover as you enjoy every moment of sexual ecstasy.

2.) Be Romantic To Your Spouse

Instead of starting your day by demonising your wife through verbal and nonverbal actions. You can actually choose to start your day by being a blessing to her. Early in the morning while in bed embrace her tightly. Kiss and tell her that you love her so much. Appreciate her through verbal and nonverbal communication. Shower her with praises. Show love and kindness to her. This in itself will trigger some excitement in her mind and prepare her for that exclusive encounter with you later at night. The way you treat your wife will definitely have either a negative or positive impact on the quality of sexual intercourse you have with her. You can therefore determine the quality of sex you would like to experience dependent on the manner in which you treat your wife. The key to your maximum sexual satisfaction lies with you. As I mentioned somewhere in this book, find below some tips;

3.) Greet your spouse by giving her a passionate kiss on her ear, neck and lips.

4.) Tell her that you love her. Verbalise it and Say some nice things to her.

5.) Eat breakfast together. Give her a light Kiss on her lips and on the forehead as you say goodbye before you go for work.

6.) Don't forget to communicate to her during the day. Send her some sweet love text messages and talk to her on the phone.

As you are about to knock off informing her that you are now leaving for home. Let her know in advance when to expect you home. Before you knock off from work remember to buy her a gift/present, a rose flower etc. Make it a point that she is ever on your mind. As soon as you reach home hug her and be with her. Give her a listening ear. Let her share with you how her day was. Be empathetic to her. Help out with some house chores. Don't just rush to TV room or bury your head in the newspaper. Remember she is your companion. Anything that is not appreciated loses value. If you buy a new car today and fail to maintain it, before long, it will lose its value and become a wreck. In the same manner any relationship that is neglected and not nurtured will definitely lose its value/meaning of existence. It will become obsolete, grow cold or become lukewarm. This principle applies also to marriage. Most marriages nowadays are going through turmoil and leave much to be desired because of neglect from both husband and wife. This problem is compounded especially when a couple starts to have children, then financial pressure begin to take its toll on marriage. Therefore, I urge both husband and wife to do everything within their power to nurture their marriage. Romance is the perfume/spice of marriage. It is the game changer to a dying, weak and lukewarm relationship.

EROTIC ENCOUNTER PREPARATION

The sexual arousal sensor for a man is activated in a totally different way compared to that of a woman. Man is sexually aroused within seconds through sight of a nude woman, picture of a naked woman. While a woman's sexual sensor takes long to be activated. She is sexually aroused through touch/sensual feelings in erotic areas and through affection.

LOVE MAKING

This is the most important intimate sexual activity in the life of a couple. It is a time when as lovers you engage in pleasurable sexual activities such as kissing, cuddling, fondling or caressing each other. It's the convergence zone of passionate sexual intercourse: intimate sexual activities which eventually lead to a point of no return of full blown, intense, pleasurable sexual explosion. This is the ultimate sexual fulfillment. When you enter your bedroom don't switch off the lights. You can make sure to play some soft love songs in the background. Take off your clothes and ensure to remain in your birth suit.

At this point, the husband should actually be very careful not to climax too early, but wait **for his wife to climax first** then continue to thrust his penis inside the vagina so that the **wife can have multiple intense orgasms.** He must **exercise full control of ejaculation** and this will eventually help the wife reach an ecstatic state of orgasm. It is a state where a woman feels an ecstasy as though in suspense of cloud 9 as she reaches the climax of sexual pleasure with loud cries of excitement. With proper timing the husband at this point can as well join in by ejaculating as he reaches the climax which is a point of no return causing an orgasmic mind blowing, breathe taking explosion. This is an apex of sexual excitement, where almost every part of the body feels good and it is at this point when his wife can make a claim of any promise the husband made in past and it is likely to be granted .

What follows is an afterglow, it is a relief and peace unspeakable, bubbling with joy inside their hearts signifying contentment. Two souls in sexual union experiencing total sexual satisfaction. What a mystery! It is indeed a blissful experience enjoyed by both a loving husband and his submissive wife. Therefore, without sexual intercourse there is no consummation of marriage.

EROGENOUS ZONES OF A WOMAN'S BODY

See Figure 3 on page 145

"An erogenous zone is an area of the body which is hyper sensitive when sexually stimulated. These areas of the body have a concentration of nerve endings. According to online Wikipedia, erogenous zones may be classified by the type of sexual response that they generate".

Basically, the entire human body is erogenous, because people differ in the manner in which they respond to sexual arousal. For instance, when a person is touched on an area of the body perceived to be erogenous depending on the mood of the person the touch may either produce sexually stimulated feelings or an irritation. Hence, what may be sexually stimulating to one may be an irritation to the other. Find below some selected erogenous zones of the woman's body;

- **LIPS**

The lips have numerous sensitive nerve endings and very delicate to touch. Therefore, tenderly kissing each other with your spouse can produce sensational sexual feelings or arousal.

- **EARS**

The inside of ears contain numerous sensory receptors, and the outer skin is also very sensitive. When you gently kiss and nibble on the lobe of an ear it can be a turn on.

- **NECK**

Nape of the neck or at the back of the neck when caressed with fingernails it can produce a stimulating feeling.

- **SCALP**

The scalp is another neglected area which can cause some goose bumps. Lightly massage the temples and with your hands run through the hair, gently tug it. This can make your partner feel so good.

- **BREASTS**

The breasts is full of sensory nerve endings which can result in sensational sexual feelings when gently stroked on the sides.

- **NIPLES**

The nipples are very sensitive to touch so don't roughly squeeze them, but be gentle and tender as you kiss, fondle and caress them. In some women it can easily respond by being rubbed or sucked.

- **INNER WRIST**

This area is a focal point of nerve endings and so it can produce some stimulating sensation when softly kissed and licked.

- **FINGERTIPS**

When holding hands or gently caressing them it can produce some sensational feelings which can lead to sexual arousal.

- **PALM**

The palm of the hand, especially the center is tender and nerve-rich. It can be guided to fondle and caress breasts, vulva and other erogenous areas of the body.

- **THIGH**

The thighs, especially the inner sides are very sensitive to touch which can stimulate sexual feelings.

- **LOWER BACK**

The lower back which is also known as the sacrum (a triangular bone in the lower back formed from fused vertebrae and situated between the two hip bones of the pelvis) is an area of the body which is sensitive to sexual stimulation.

- ## **LOWER ABDOMEN**

This is an area just under the belly button. It responds very well to soft touches which can make a woman feel pleasurable.

- ## **BUTTOCKS**

The buttocks are among the primary erogenous zones of the female body.

- ## **VAGINA**

A word of caution: The vagina is the most erogenous area, but it needs total care, patience, and gentleness before being penetrated. Husbands should learn to handle this organ with tender care. It should be treated like a flower because it is fragile.

- ## **CLITORIS**

The clitoris is the most sensitive area of the female sexual organs. Since it is extremely sensitive, it's the easiest and fastest way for a woman to reach orgasm.

- ## **G-SPOT**

The G. Spot when properly stimulated, may cause intense sexual arousal, powerful orgasms and can make a woman squirt (female ejaculation) uncontrollably.

WHAT A WOMAN NEEDS TO KNOW ABOUT A MAN'S SEXUALITY

A man unlike a woman is sexually aroused through sight and touch (feelings). Usually men enjoy feasting on nude pictures and videos. They get turned on. Often times Prostitutes like to capitalize on this attribute. They are generally in the habit of using this tactic of exposing their nudity in order to seduce men. Hence this tactic can also be used by wives to lure their husbands for sex. Women should be sexually attractive to their own husbands.

Therefore, during love making a woman should make sure that she is wearing see-through clothes exposing her beautiful and attractive body to her husband. Sex to man is as important as food is to him, hence a woman ought to be wise not to deprive him of this important need. When a man is sexually excited, he will become restless until sex is given to him. He will start demanding and pleading with the wife for sex. He loses interest in ordinary food, sleep or any other thing until sex is given to him. He won't quit in making such demands. He will even use different tactics to compel the wife to give him sex. Tactics such as being nice, loving and more affectionate to her. When a man is sexually excited he can make far-fetched promises to his wife just for him to have sex.

A word of caution to women, please avoid borrowing or receiving gifts or favours of any kind from some men. Especially someone who is not your relative, fiancée or husband. Don't be naïve because some men are very subtle. They can continue to shower you with gifts and favours until you become entangled in their trap. Eventually, you become indebted to them and end up giving in to their selfish demands because it is almost impossible for you to pay them back. When you fail to pay them back they will ask or demand sexual favours from you.

Naturally, a woman's heart can easily be won by a romantic and loving man who knows how to be kind and affectionate to a woman. Women are not difficult to love, just the act of bringing her flowers can easily exhilarate her. Most women often times get swept off their feet by such romantic men. It is actually easy for a loving husband to have his sexual need met by his wife as long as he continues to love her dearly.

EROGENOUS ZONES OF A MAN'S BODY

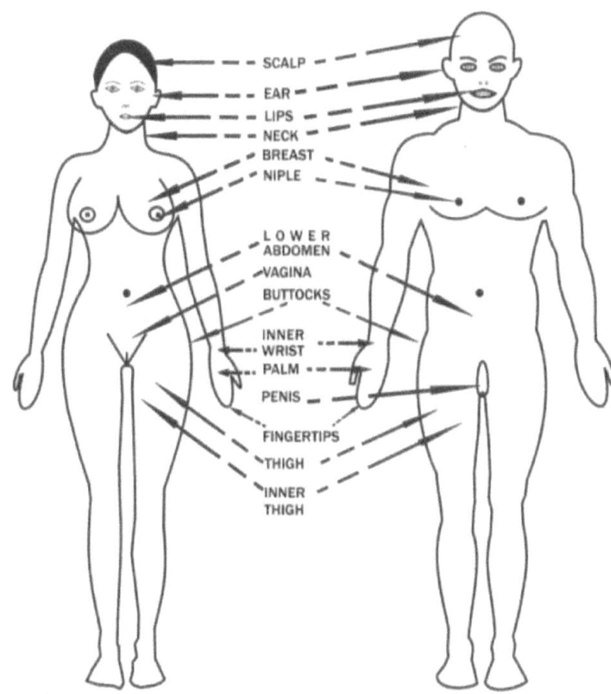

Figure 3: Erogenous zones of a man & a woman's body

- **PENIS**

The penis is one of the most male erogenous zones. Men can be aroused sexually through the stimulation of the penile shaft.

- **GLANS**

The glans especially its upper sides can cause arousal in men through thorough stimulation.

- **SCROTUM**

The scrotum is one of men's most erogenous areas. The scrotum has numerous nerves and it is hyper sensitive to touch.

- **PERINEUM**

The perineum is located between the behind of scrotum and the anus. It holds the male's ejaculatory muscles.

- **FRENULUM**

The frenulum is the ridge below the head of the penis. It is an area located on the underside of the glans. It is very sensitive to touch and can arouse a man's sexual feelings.

- **LIPS**

The lips have numerous sensitive nerve endings and very delicate to touch. Therefore, tenderly kissing each other with your spouse can produce sensational sexual feelings or arousal.

- **EARS**

The inside of ears contain numerous sensory receptors, and the outer skin is also very sensitive. When you gently kiss and nibble on the lobe of an ear it can be a turn on.

- **NECK**

Nape of the neck or at the back of the neck when caressed with fingernails it can produce a stimulating feeling.

- **SCALP**

The scalp is another neglected area which can cause some goose bumps. Lightly massage the temples and with your hands run through the hair, gently tug it. This can make your partner feel so good.

- **LOWER BACK**

The lower back which is also known as the sacrum (a triangular bone in the lower back formed from fused vertebrae and situated between the two hip bones of the pelvis) is an area of the body which is sensitive to sexual stimulation.

- **LOWER ABDOMEN**

This is an area just under the belly button. It responds very well to soft touches which can make a man feel pleasurable.

- **BUTTOCKS**

The buttocks are among the primary erogenous zones of the male body.

- **NIPLES**

The nipples are very sensitive to touch so don't roughly squeeze them, but be gentle and tender as you kiss, fondle and caress them.

- **INNER WRIST**

This area is a focal point of nerve endings and so it can produce some stimulating sensation when softly kissed and licked.

- **FINGERTIPS**

When holding hands or gently caressing them it can produce some sensational feelings which can lead to sexual arousal.

- **PALM**

The palm of the hand, especially the center is tender and nerve-rich. It can be guided to fondle and caress penis and other erogenous areas of the male body.

- **THIGH**

The thighs, especially the inner sides are very sensitive to touch which can stimulate sexual feelings.

HOW TO BRING BACK
ROMANCE IN
YOUR MARRIAGE

Find below some tips on how to bring back romance in your marriage;

i) Help change your wife's wardrobe regularly; by buying her new clothes and shoes which are fashionable. Nowadays, you can buy nice clothes and shoes which are fashionable and affordable.

ii) Include her in your budget regularly for her hairdo and make up.

iii) As a wife make sure that you do everything possible to look attractive to your husband. Wear clothes which are revealing/see through when you are the two of you in your living room/bedroom. *"And they were both naked, the man and his wife, and were not ashamed."* **Genesis 2:25**

iv) Tell your wife verbally that you love her, and affirm or show it through your actions that you truly love her. If you don't someone else will do it.

v) Spend quality time with your wife. Have an interrupted conversation and listen to her attentively.

vi) Have fun with your spouse, laugh, kiss, and cuddle or embrace each other in the privacy of your home without any expectation of sex on your mind.

"Let his left hand be under my head And his right hand embrace me."
Song of Solomon 2:6

CHAPTER NINE

SEX TECHNIQUES AND
SEXUAL FULFILMENT

PREMATURE EJACULATION

PREMATURE EJACULATION (PE): Is the ejaculation of semen by a man during sexual intercourse either before or immediately after penetration. The consensus of experts at the International Society for Sexual Medicine endorsed a definition of premature ejaculation as around one minute after penetration.

However, for various reasons some men just can't control their ejaculation. The major contributing factor to this dilemma can be attributed to a number of health challenges some men face. The fact that some men have been grappling with this challenge for years doesn't mean that nothing can done to bring about some improvement in this area .

In men's circles early ejaculation or release is a symbol or mark of manhood. As we were growing up elderly men would encourage us as young men to actually demonstrate our manhood whenever we have a sexual encounter with our wives. We have grown up to believe that a man should always demonstrate dominance over a lady sexually. He has to subdue and conquer a woman in bed. This attitude has greatly contributed to a big problem of premature ejaculation a lot of men are facing, because they would want to prove a point that they are real men and can sexually satisfy their women in bed with easy.

Naturally, men's sexual response is quicker than that of women. However, most men mistaken their ability to respond quickly to sexual stimulation to imply that they are real men capable of satisfying their lovers within minutes. They mistakenly believe that a quick release is a symbol of masculinity. They think that their sexual power and dominance lies in quick sexual response which results in premature ejaculation. Most men prematurely ejaculate as soon as they reach a point of no return-orgasm. At this point they have no control over ejaculation. Depending on a particular man's sensitivity or degree of intensity of sexual stimulation can either ejaculate before or after penetration. As soon as a man releases he loses his sexual urge. While all this is happening in a man's dominance world the interest of a woman is completely ignored. They don't care about sexually fulfilling their wives.

Men are generally preoccupied by the goose pumps or enjoyment that comes with the very act of sexual intercourse. It is in the process of lovemaking that some men unexpectedly lose control of ejaculation. The moment one ejaculates there is no turning back. There is absolutely nothing that one can do to stop the process of ejaculation. Immediately after ejaculation and having a 'thrilling' experience of orgasm the husband loses interest in sex. He falls asleep and starts to snore while his wife is fuming with anger by his side. **Ed and Gaye Wheat in their book 'Intended for pleasure' said, "Not only is the wife denied the feeling of sexual release in orgasm, but she may also have acute and chronic physical pain stemming from congestion of her pelvic organs, engorged with blood that is normally released with orgasm."**

The problem of premature ejaculation has brought misery and frustrations to many wives in marriages. This problem has adversely affected the sex drive of many women. The ego of womanhood is terribly crashed such that wives are left without hope. Imagine, you as a wife making a lifelong pledge and commitment to your beloved husband, to remain faithful and royal to him. In fact you both agree to forsake all others and exclusively meet each other's sexual needs in the confines of your marriage.

Reality, then dawns on you that the problem your husband is grappling with is actually a nightmare and insurmountable than you thought because it may eventually lead to impotence. When suddenly you encounter such a challenge in your marriage, what do you do? Do you discard your marriage vows and seek conjugal services elsewhere? How do you mitigate such a challenge?

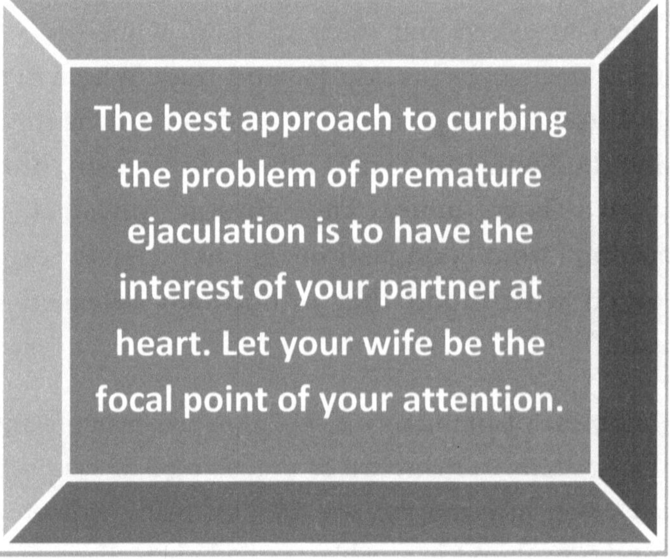

The best approach to curbing the problem of premature ejaculation is to have the interest of your partner at heart. Let your wife be the focal point of your attention. Since it takes long for a woman to respond sexually, spend more time warming her up. No matter how aroused you become learn to defer your pleasure to a later time.

It is very important for any man to learn about a woman's sexuality. Know your wife's erogenous zones. In your quest to pleasure her sexually don't rush into fondling, touching and caressing her more sensitive sexual organs, because your actions can become an irritation and may put her off. Start with the peripherals first such as massaging her back, boobs, legs, feet, fingers, hands, palms, neck, ear lobes, tracing her face, hair and etc. This will make her feel emotionally connected with you. As you progress in your lovemaking go deeper into fondling and kissing her breasts and nipples. In the midst of all this continue with verbal and non-verbal communication, ask questions and let her guide your hand to certain body parts of her liking.

Mind you, her arousal is gradual so make sure to be alert and observant. Be keen to look for signs of arousal - her breathing changes, her breasts and nipples swell. Her vagina swells and tightens ready to receive the penis. This is now the right time to kiss her passionately, fondle her inner thighs, while gently touching/stroking her clitoris and its surround area. At this time everything is permissible as long as none of the partners is offended. You can as well use lubricating oil to gently rub her clitoris with your fingers until she bergs you to enter her. Even though you see these signs continue to stimulate her sensitive organs with gentleness.

When you insert your penis inside her vagina remember to observe a moment of silence in order to avoid early ejaculation. Let the communication lines remain open. She should as well reduce her pelvic movements in order to allow you to gain momentum. However, as soon as you gain control start thrusting your manhood with vigor and embrace each other tightly. If you synchronize so well you can experience orgasms almost at the same time.

The size of the penis is immaterial, no matter how small it is as long as it remains firm and able to do its function accordingly the better. However, it is impossible for a flaccid penis to penetrate a vagina and also ejaculate. When a woman is fully aroused sexually the vagina releases some slippery secretions (fluid). The purpose of this secretion is to act as a lubricant in order to prepare the vagina to receive the penis and also allow smooth movement of the sperm during sexual intercourse.

CAUSES OF PRMATURE EJACULATION

Premature Ejaculation can be caused by a number of different emotional and physical factors such as:

i) When a man becomes too excited sexually

ii) A very sensitive penis

iii) Nervousness.

iv) Stress

v) Depression

vi) Relationship problems

vii) Performance related anxiety

viii) Diabetes

ix) High blood pressure

x) Thyroid problems or prostate disease

xi) Low levels of serotonin in the brain

EJACULATION CONTROL TECHNIQUES

THE PAUSE-SQUEEZE TECHNIQUE

The Pause-Squeeze technique is a procedure that must be practiced often during foreplay in order for the husband to gain full control of ejaculation. The moment you feel you are about to ejaculate, signal to your partner to squeeze the end of your penis where the head (glans) joins the shaft. The wife must press her thumb on the underside of the husband's penis, a few inches below the slit or opening of the penis. While her two fingers must be placed on the opposite side of the penis, with one finger above the ridge and the other just below ridge. Non-verbal or physical communication must be used when the husband is about to ejaculate.

A signal must be communicated to the wife so that she applies pressure by squeezing the head of the penis with her two fingers and the thumb together for about four seconds until the husband loses the urge to ejaculate and wait for fifteen to thirty seconds and continue with the same process for four to five seconds of the twenty minutes session. Your wife can hold the squeeze on the head of your penis for several seconds until your arousal slows down.

The Pause-Squeeze Control technique procedure when practiced thoroughly may become a solution to heightened sexual pleasure for any couple desiring a thrilling sexual relationship.

STRENGTHENING THE PUBUCOCCYGEUS (P.C.) MUSCLE

Strengthening your pelvic floor muscle is of critical importance to having maximum sexual fulfillment in marriage. Actually, just before the point of ejaculation, you are able to squeeze and tighten your Pubucoccygeus (P.C.) muscles, and continue in sexual intercourse. Since you are in control of ejaculation due to a strong Pubucoccygeus (P.C.) muscle you are able to concentrate on helping your wife reach orgasm during sexual intercourse.

Dr. Arnold H. Kegel, a surgeon and professor of gynecology at the University Of Southern California School Of Medicine, in the early 1940s, made a discovery about women who had trouble controlling urine flow when coughing, laughing or sneezing. This problem also referred to as urinary stress incontinence. However, it was discovered that strengthening the Pubucoccygeus (P.C.) muscle could help control the flow of urine.

These exercises are called Kegel exercises. Kegel exercises are critical to strengthening the P. C. muscle group for both men and women. In men a weak P. C muscle is the cause of premature ejaculation and in women it is one of the causes of orgasmic dysfunction. Orgasmic dysfunction is when a woman fails to reach orgasm during sexual intercourse for a couple of reasons. Generally, it could be due to a woman's negative attitude and thoughts about sex. Therefore, the change in attitude and thoughts, and also the strengthening and toning of P. C. muscle is cardinal to improving sexual satisfaction in both men and women.

LOCATION OF THE PUBUCOCCYGEUS (P.C.) MUSCLES

The P. C. muscle group is suspended between two solid non-moving bony structures. They are positioned above the legs and extend from the pubic bone to coccyx (tailbone) in both male and female human body. They form the floor of the pelvis or abdominal pelvic cavity, and its primary purpose is supporting the abdominal and pelvic organs, and control of urinary flow. It is the central and primary component of three muscles that make up a muscle group called the levator **ani**. The levator ani is a broad, thin muscle, situated on either side of the pelvis. It is formed from three muscle components: the pubococcygeus, the iliococcygeus, and the puborectalis. It is attached to the inner surface of each side of the lesser pelvis, and these unite to form the greater part of the pelvic floor.

PELVIC FLOOR MUSCLES

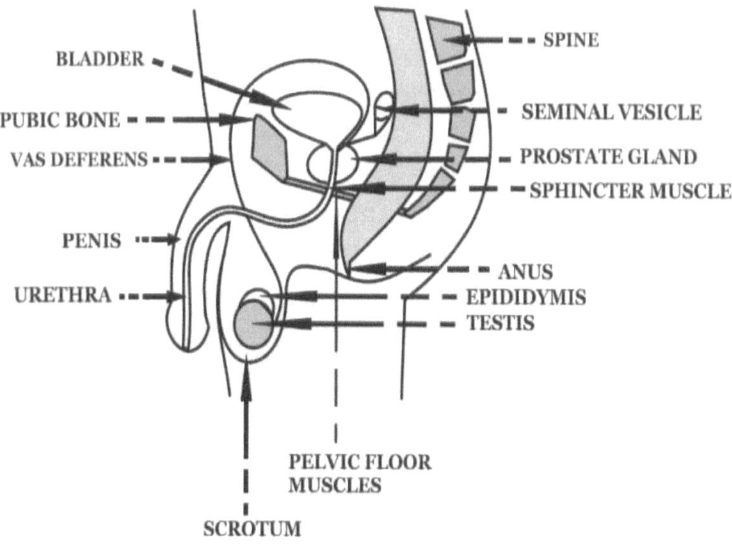

Figure 4: Pelvic Floor Muscles

THE PUBUCOCCYGEUS (P.C.) MUSCLE/ KEGEL EXERCISES

The Kegel exercises can be practiced by both husband and wife as partners. It is important that you take time to make sure you are exercising the right muscles, so be patient with yourself.

When you learn precisely how to contract the P. C. muscle you can begin an exercise program. Your goal should be to do 20 contractions of Kegel exercises three to four times each day as a minimum and slowly increase the number of times per day. You strengthen your pelvic floor muscle by holding the contraction for two seconds, and then relax for three to four seconds. Please! Don't stress yourself when you are just starting. You can start with five to ten contractions when you wake up and every time you pee by holding each contraction for only two seconds.

After four days of exercises when you gain confidence that you are exercising the right muscle you can then do ten contractions of Kegel exercises six times per day. Since each contraction takes two seconds, it will then mean that the total time of exercises will only take two minutes per day. It can take six to ten weeks or longer to strengthen your pelvic floor muscle. It actually takes regular exercises and time to strengthen them. The more you do them, the stronger your P. C. muscles will become. After six weeks you can do 20 contractions of Kegel exercises for 20 to 30 times in a day which will only take on average twenty minutes per day.

You can do your Kegel exercises before you wake up in the morning, in the afternoon and evening. You can as well do the Kegel exercises while sitting, standing or walking, especially when your muscles get stronger. Avoid holding your breath or tightening your stomach, buttock or thigh muscles at the same time. When your P. C. muscle is strengthened you will be able to control ejaculation with easy and overcome incontinence or urine leakage without seeking medication or surgery. Kegel exercises are very important as such should be incorporated into your lifestyle. Remember, that just as it takes time to build biceps and strengthen any other muscle in your body, it takes time to strengthen muscles in your pelvic floor, hence the need for regular practice.

HOW DO I KNOW IAM EXERCISING THE PELVIC MUSCLES?

i) When you stand to urinate (pee) with knees spread, try to stop and start your urine flow. If urination is interrupted then the P. C. muscles have been contracted.

ii) You can know if you see the perineum rises. The perineum is the area between the anus and the vagina opening/ the penis.

iii) You can know by placing a finger about an inch and a half inside the vagina and feel the muscle contract.

BENEFITS OF A STRENGTHENED PUBUCOCCYGEUS (P.C.) MUSCLE

- ✓ The support of pelvic organs is improved.
- ✓ Improvement in urinary control.
- ✓ Improved ejaculation control in men.
- ✓ A woman is able to voluntarily contract the P. C.
- ✓ The vagina is able to grip the penis tightly
- ✓ A wife is able to reach orgasm with easy
- ✓ Sexual fulfillment is guaranteed.
- ✓ Injuries are minimalized during childbirth.
- ✓ Safety of both mother and baby during birth process
- ✓ Natural childbirth becomes effective.

The human body is generally covered with a number of nerve endings which are sensitive to light touch, but the nerve endings in the P. C. muscles are actually sensitive to pressure. The vagina is however, surrounded by these pressure-sensitive nerve endings of the P. C. muscles.

Therefore, for greater sexual stimulation the penis inside the vagina must be subjected to a firm squeezing pressure originating from strong P. C. muscles. But the vagina which is surrounded by a weak P. C. muscle group will not have the strength to exert pressure on the penis for sexual stimulation. Even though a large object is inserted inside the vagina it won't increase sexual sensitivity for the wife, since sensitivity depends on contraction of the P. C. muscles and not stretching. Hence, the size of the penis has got nothing to do with the wife's sensitivity.

The wife's sensitivity during sexual intercourse is often as a result of the contraction of a strong P. C. muscle group accompanied by the thrusting of the penis inside a tight vagina.

The secret that will drive a woman crazy sexually is basically a tight vagina due to a strong P. C. muscle group. Therefore stop looking down upon your husband, but instead engage yourself in Kegel exercises to improve the strength of your P. C. muscles. Complaining and heaping insults on your husband as the cause of your orgasmic dysfunctional won't help, but the complete paradigm shift necessitated by change of attitude and perception about sex will do.

SEXUAL POSITIONS
AND TECHNIQUES

Delicious sex is very important, just like delicious food. Sex is a very important aspect of a healthy marriage relationship. In fact God has made us different from all animals and other creatures. We have been fearfully and wonderfully made. Our physical bodies have been uniquely designed to engage in a variety of sex positions. There is no limit in terms of sex positions, we can explore as many sex styles as possible as long as it pleases God and our partner. **What is forbidden is sexual pervasion as explained in chapter 6.**

Find below a list of a few common sex positions.

1.) **WOMAN ON TOP**: Is a sex position in which the husband lies on his back with his legs closed, while the wife straddles him in a kneeling position facing either forward or backward. Then an erect penis is inserted by either the husband or his wife into the vagina.

The advantages of this position are as follows;

a) It is easier to stimulate the clitoris.

   i) A woman has control over the rhythm, pace of vaginal stimulation, extent and duration of penetration.

ii) This position makes the wife more active.

iii) She can as well massage her husband's scrotum.

2.) **MISSIONARY OR MAN ON TOP SEX POSITION**: Is a sex position in which generally a wife lies on her back and a husband lies on top of her while facing each other and engage in vaginal intercourse. The advantages of this position are as follows;

a) It is romantic

b) The couple is able to look into each other's eyes

c) The couple is able to kiss and caress each other

d) It is considered as a good position for reproduction.

e) This position allows the husband to control the rhythm and depth of pelvic thrusting.

f) In this position the wife can thrust against her husband by moving her hips or squeeze him closer with her arms or legs.

3.) **SIDE BY SIDE/LATERAL POSITION**: This is a sex position in which the husband lies on his left side facing his wife and the wife lies on her right side facing her husband. Then his wife puts her right leg between his legs and placing her left leg over his right leg. In fact you can start with man on top-missionary position, then roll to your sides, husband on his left side and the wife on her right.

The advantages of this position are as follows;

a) Each partner has at least one hand free for caressing and fondling.

b) Each partner is free to thrust or move hips.

c) Each partner is not pinned down by the weight of the other.

4.) **STANDING SEX POSITION**: Is a sex position in which the husband holds his wife's thighs and she wraps her legs around his waist whilst with her hands embracing him around his neck. Then the husband lifts her up so that with one hand he can insert his penis into her vagina and continue to firmly hold her thighs. Please note, both the husband and wife must be strong enough to engage in this sex position so as to avoid unnecessary accidents.

5.) **KNEELING SEX POSITION**: Is a sex position in which the husband kneels down on bed first and then his wife facing him, she wraps her legs around his waist whilst with her hands embracing him around his neck.

The advantage of this position is that the couple can kiss, fondle, caress and embrace each other passionately.

6.) **ARMLESS CHAIR OR SEATED SEX POSITION**: Is a sex position in which the husband seats on an armless chair and his wife seats on his lap facing him, carefully inserts an erect penis into her vagina.

The advantage of this position is that the couple can kiss, fondle, caress and embrace each other tightly.

7.) **REAR-ENTRY POSITION:** It is a sex position in which the husband enters his wife's vagina from behind. The husband can do this either in a kneeling or standing position.

The advantage of this position is that it is good for deep penetration.

CHAPTER TEN

HOW TO GIVE YOUR SPOUSE
MIND BLOWING ORGASMS

THE FOUR SEXUAL RESPONSE CYCLE

The human sexual response cycle is a four-stage model of physiological responses to sexual stimulation. According to their order of occurrence, are as follows; the excitement, plateau, orgasm and resolution phases. This physiological response model was first formulated by William H. Masters and Virginia E. Johnson (1915 – 2001), and 1925).

Two Basic Physiological Response are as follows;

i)   Vasocongestion (Penile and Clitoral erection, breasts)

ii) Myotonia (Flexion and contraction of muscles)

THE FOUR – PHASE MODEL

i)   Excitement

ii)   Plateau

iii) Orgasm

iv)   Resolution

PHASE 1-EXCITEMENT

It is in this phase when the couple is trying to arouse their sexual feelings. Gradually, their sexual desire (libido) is aroused. This phase is a very important part of the sexual process, because it is a time when a couple is closed up in seclusion from the outside world. In as far as things are concerned during this time everyone else is not as important as your spouse.

This is the time to give your lover undivided attention. It is the time when you literally adore the one you love. You adore your lover as you get lost in his/her presence. You need nothing, but cherish, enjoy and express profound love to your spouse. You love and enjoy every moment with your lover. Everything else doesn't make sense at all as you enjoy the company and presence of each other. You fall in the arms of your lover and hold each other tightly, but gently.

All this is done when you are just the two of you as love birds in the privacy of your home. The environment or atmosphere should be attractive and conducive for love making free from any form of disturbance or intrusion.

In fact it makes good sense as a precondition to take a bath before the act of sex. This in itself will mean that you care for each other and truly value the act itself. Make the art of lovemaking enjoyable. Don't be rough as a man, but tender, gentle and affectionate. You can gently touch her breast while kissing her. Touch her boobs/buttocks and let her be your instructor to guide you where to touch and which area of her body to explore.

When making love remember to talk to each other. Communication is key during love making. When a woman has been aroused fully there are signs to look for to show you her readiness for penetration. Even though you see these signs wait until she begs you to penetrate her.

PHASE 2-THE PLATEAU STAGE

The plateau phase is the period of sexual excitement prior to orgasm. It is a time when blood circulation and heart rate in both male and female is increased, with increased sexual pleasure and increased stimulation and there is also an increased muscle tension, and respiration also continues at an elevated level. Involuntary vocalization in both sexes happens at this stage. Sexual frustration may be experienced when there is a prolonged time without progression into the orgasmic phase.

MALES IN PLATEAU STAGE: The male urethral sphincter contracts thereby preventing urine from mixing with seminal fluid and also ensures that retrograde ejaculation doesn't happen. The muscles at the base of the penis begin a steady rhythmic contraction and this may cause the secretion of seminal fluid, and the testicles rise closer to the body.

FEMALES IN PLATEAU STAGE:

During this stage the clitoris becomes very sensitive and withdraws slightly, lubrication is produced further. The outer third tissues of the vagina swell, and the pubococcygeus muscles tightens, hence reducing the diameter of the opening of the vagina. This reduction in size causes the vagina to grip the penis.

PHASE 3-ORGASM

An orgasm is the climax or peak of sexual excitement, during the sexual response cycle, characterized by intensely pleasurable and sensational feelings around the genital area. Actually, in men involuntary contractions, muscle tension and finally an ejaculation-a release, emission or discharge of seminal fluid and semen occurs. While, in women involuntary Rhythmic contractions of the lower third of the vagina occurs. Within a second, a woman can experience from three to ten contractions and it has been described as a momentary feeling of suspension-an ecstasy, followed by a sensation of warmth starting in the perineum area and pervading the entire body.

According to an online article by Melinda Wenner of Scienceline, a project of New York University's Science, Health and Environmental Reporting Program, dated 1st February, 2013. Research, using positron emission tomography (PET) scans has shown that in order for a person to reach orgasm, a primary requirement is to let go of all fear and anxiety. Then there is the biochemistry of orgasm itself. Research shows that during ejaculation, men release a cocktail of brain chemicals, including norepinephrine, serotonin, oxytocin, vasopressin, Nitric oxide (NO), and the hormone prolactin. The release of prolactin is linked to the feeling of sexual satisfaction.

PHASE 4-RELAXATION/RESOLUTION

In the relaxation stage both husband and wife would want to relax. However, it is always natural for the husband to fall asleep immediately after sex, but it is not so with a woman. It is very irritating and annoying to the wife whenever her husband falls asleep and starts to snore. This attitude on the part of the husband leaves the wife feeling uncared for and used as a mere sex object. There is need for a complete paradigm shift on the part of the husband for the sake of his dear wife. Instead of falling asleep immediately after sex the husband should continue to converse, caress, and fondle his wife lovingly, until the fires and passion of lovemaking and orgasm dies down to a calm relaxation.

According to an online article by Melinda Wenner of Scienceline, a project of New York University's Science, Health and Environmental Reporting Program, dated 1st February, 2013, entitled, 'Why Do Guys Get Sleepy After Sex?' In this article she reports that research has shown that there are multiple factors that contribute to post-coitus sleep. Prolactin levels are naturally higher during sleep, and animals injected with the chemical become tired immediately. This suggests a strong link between prolactin and sleep, so it's likely that the hormone's release during orgasm causes men to feel sleepy.

Oxytocin and vasopressin, two other chemicals released during orgasm, are also associated with sleep. Their release frequently accompanies that of melatonin, the primary hormone that regulates our body clocks. Oxytocin is also thought to reduce stress levels, which again could lead to relaxation and sleepiness.

THE ART OF LOVEMAKING

The act of sex: love making and fulfillment of sexual intimacy in human beings is a process which ought not to be rushed or done in a hurry. Remember, the goal and objective of this act of love is to ultimately achieve maximum sexual pleasure for both husband and wife. In order for the married couple to achieve this they both need the full involvement and cooperation of each other. No spouse is permitted to just be a spectator, but ought to be a participant to make the whole process successful and enjoyable.

The art of lovemaking or process can be likened to any recipe. If a married couple is to ultimately achieve the maximum sexual satisfaction from the holy act of sex then the whole process of love making (recipe of sex) must be followed and adhered to religiously, in order to produce the desired outcome or results of each phase of the sexual response cycle; the expected desired outcome namely; excitement, plateau, orgasm and resolution or relaxation.

The scriptures from the holy bible says that the marriage bed should be kept pure and honoured by all. The act of sex is a very important component in the life of any God-fearing couple and as such it needs to be treated with respect and honour. Anything that we value in life must not be neglected, but ought to ensure that it is on top of our list of priorities. Therefore if you are to get the best out of the act sex, then plan for it.

Find below essential nuggets to an effective and enjoyable intimate sexual relationship between husband and wife. These nuggets will ensure that the married couple gets maximum fulfilment from the holy act of sex.

a) **TIME:** Time is of essence if we are to enjoy and achieve a quality relationship with our spouse. It is of paramount importance to any married couple to plan their sexual activity. Come up with a time table and set goals to guide you on when, where and how to do your sexual activity.

   Bishop Dr. Joe Imakando said that, ***"Life on this side of eternity is so short that it must be lived within one's clear purpose and goals."***

b) **PRIVACY:** In order for a couple to derive maximum sexual satisfaction from their intimate relationship, an ideal and private place is crucial. Hence the need for any married couple to plan in advance for their dream house to have a self-contained bedroom which will provide the necessary privacy to enable them enjoy themselves fully without any outside disturbance.

c) **HYGIENE:** According to the World Health Organization, "Hygiene refers to conditions and practices that help to maintain health and prevent the spread of diseases." Someone said cleanliness is next to Godliness. It is very important for any married couple to observe hygienic practices. I recommend a bath early in the mornings and evenings precisely before a couple engages in sex.

d) **SKILL:** Skill is the ability to do something well; expertise. In most of our African setting as soon as a girl reaches puberty information or knowledge pertaining to their womanhood is quickly passed on to them so as to equip and prepare them for marriage as soon as they become adults. But it is not so with boys as they reach puberty. Most of them remain ignorant about marriage as a result, this makes them poor lovers when they marry in their adulthood. However, this should not be so to any married couple in this era and age. We should work hard by reading books on marriage extensively and acquire knowledge. Bishop Dr. Joe Imakando said that, "You cannot rise above the level of what you know. Lack of knowledge will limit you. It will limit what you can do and your progress in life.

e) **COMMUNICATION:** Communication is the effective and efficient exchange of information and ideas through verbal, non-verbal, written, visual and other medium. So communication is key to an exciting and enjoyable sexual relationship. Without applying an effective communication system any couple is expected to experience an unsatisfactory sexual encounter. It is therefore imperative for any couple to effectively communicate to each other during sex. Make sure to effectively communicate your sexual plans. Set goals and objectives about your sexual union. Where are you going to have it from? Is the place suitable enough to guarantee a fulfilling sexual encounter? Have a check list to ensure that everything is done according to plan. Find answers for such questions like, when, where, how, What. Is it just sex for pleasure or maybe you need a baby? If it is for pleasure then you should see to it that you are on contraceptive e.g. birth control pills or condoms or whatever type of contraceptive you may be using to avoid unwanted pregnancies.

Find below some important tips to help **husbands** achieve maximum sexual pleasure:

- Spend more time caressing her clitoris and the surrounding area.

- Always refrain from engaging in sex frequently (e.g. having sex more than once a day), but replenish your reserves by waiting for 24 hrs, before having another sexual encounter.

- Be patient with your wife no matter how aroused you are don't rush into having sexual intercourse with her before foreplay. Spend more time preparing your wife through love making.

- During orgasm you should voluntarily contract your anal sphincter muscles. Let your wife caress you especially on the underside of the penis (frenulum).

Find below some important tips to help **wives** achieve maximum sexual pleasure:

i)   **Engage your mind:** The mind is the most important and powerful sexual organ of the human body. The battle is either won or lost in the mind. Maximum Sexual fulfillment or pleasure can only become possible when we engage the mind. Your expectation can only be realized when you visualise having an enjoyable sexual encounter with your spouse before and during the actual experience.

ii)   **Be an Initiator:** Avoid inertia, don't behave like a log of wood, but be active before and during the very act of sex. He is your lover and sexual partner, so indicate to him that you enjoy it too.

iii)   **Be an active Participant:** Stop being a spectator and become an active participant in the very act of sex. So during orgasm increase the intensity of the pelvic dance/movement. This will equally enhance the intensity of sexual pleasure.

iv)   **Stop being a Workaholic:** a workaholic is a person who spends much more time working than necessary. Most wives spend much more time doing house chores than necessary. It is not bad to do house chores, but there is need to plan to enable you strike a balance and give equal time and attention to other important things in your marriage such as sex. In as much as it is important to engage yourself in doing house chores, it is also equally important not to neglect your conjugal duties as a wife. Scriptures in the holy bible says that you shouldn't defraud your spouse of sex. It is illegal to deprive your spouse of his/her conjugal rights. When you put an action plan in place you will avoid giving unnecessary excuses because you will have reserved enough energy for this special occasion and eventually save your marriage from the heartaches of infidelity.

ACTUALISING TRUE LOVE AND SEXUAL SATISFACTION

The ultimate true love and sexual fulfillment in marriage can only be actualised through the willpower. God has given us the willpower; the unwavering strength of will to carry out our wishes-visions. We are talking about the ability to have our wishes fulfilled. We have a lot of wishes: such as the wish to experience true love and a satisfying sexual relationship, but unless we decide to take action our status quo will remain the same.

Successful married couples have a strong willpower which help them pursue their dreams. They usually have the courage, tenacity and determination to birth their dreams and visions. Although, you have a hundred reasons to give up on your dreams, the moment you summon your inner willpower everything becomes possible.

The power to enjoying true love and sexual fulfillment lies within you. All that is required is a paradigm shift from self-centeredness to spouse-centeredness. Let your spouse be the centre of attention. When your spouse becomes the center of the object your love then both you and your spouse will become the beneficiaries of true love. Your spouse's interest and focus will automatically shift to you as a center of attention. Then both you and your spouse will be winners in spite of the fact that your individual focus and attention has shifted. When the center of the object of your love is directed at your spouse no one is a loser.

In the same vein, without any coercion, but with the willpower within us we are able to experience and express true love to our spouses despite our inadequacies. We can as well choose to have an ultimate sexual fulfillment in marriage through our willpower. Nothing happens by chance, but through thorough planning. To every effect there is a cause meaning that if you fail to plan then you are planning to fail.

An environment where true love abides is a product of the choices couples make every day. What we are today is as a result of the choices we made yesterday. No one can decide for you, you can have an excellent opportunity to experience true love and sexual fulfillment in your marriage, but unless you choose to do so a golden opportunity will go begging.

"See then that you walk circumspectly, not as fools but as wise, redeeming the time, because the days are evil. Therefore do not be unwise, but understand what the will of the Lord is." **Ephesians 5:15-17**

Married couples should make every effort to ensure that an ideal environment for sex is set. An ideal environment is a perfect timing when both the husband and wife are ready and fully prepared to explore and have a thrilling sexual encounter. It is actually wrong for a man to force himself on a woman before she is adequately prepared for sexual intercourse. The sexuality of men is usually different from that of women. Men are easily aroused compared to women. Men get aroused quickly just by the sight of a nude woman. So men's sexual response can be likened to a pressing iron. No sooner you switch it on than it gets hot. In other words, it becomes red hot as soon as you switch it on.

On the other hand, the sexual response of women is very slow compared to that of men. The sexual response of women can be likened to the process of making a brazier. It takes a lot of time, effort and patience before the brazier becomes red hot. In the same manner it takes a lot of time, effort and patience before a woman is aroused sexually.

Hence the need for men to be patient with women before they engage in sexual intercourse. Entering a woman before she is fully aroused sexually is tantamount to sexual abuse. When a man penetrates a woman who is not ready, the sexual act itself becomes very painful to her. Therefore, lovemaking is not necessarily the time immediately before sex, but the preparation must start early in the morning. So let your lovemaking be online all the time meaning that you have to be romantic to your spouse every moment of the day. We need to learn as men to be tender and affectionate to our women. Women take delight in being treasured and loved all the time by their spouses. The fact that she is your companion make it a point as a husband to draw closer to her even during her menstruation or menopause because this is the period when there is a swing or an imbalance in her hormonal system. It is during this period when women become emotionally disturbed and need the companionship of their spouse the most.

THE IMPORTANCE OF FEMALE ORGASM

Basically, when the bible says that don't deprive one another of sex, it acknowledges the fact that both the husband and wife have sexual needs. Therefore, each spouse should take responsibility to ensure that their partner is fully satisfied sexually. Certainly, the husband should always realise that his wife has a sexual need. This sexual need can be dissected into three important segments such as the need for **affection, sexual release** and **sexual pleasure.**

THE NEED FOR AFFECTION

What is affection? According to www.merriamwebster.com, Affection is a feeling of liking and caring for someone: tender attachment: Fondness.

If a woman is to enjoy sex or get satisfied sexually certainly there is need to set the conditions right. In order to achieve this the woman should first experience true romance or affection. She should feel that tender care and loving from her husband. She should occupy the first and most important slot in the heart and mind of her husband. All the tenderness and fondness ought to be directed at her and her alone. The moment this condition is met the probability of her experiencing mind blowing orgasms is 100%.

The Need For Sexual Release

When a woman is aroused during sexual intercourse the act shouldn't be aborted prematurely before she experiences an orgasm. Actually, what happens when a woman is aroused during sexual intercourse is that all the sexual organs in the pelvic area get engorged or saturated with blood and a sexual release can only happen during an orgasm. When a woman fails to reach an orgasm she will experience pain in the lower back and the pelvic area.

The need for sexual pleasure

Sexual intimacy between husband and wife is according to God's own beautiful design. It is the glue that cements the very fabric of marriage. It is through sexual intimacy that the one flesh principle is fulfilled.

Actually, there is no need for any woman not to experience an orgasm during sexual intercourse. This is so because a woman's body was specifically designed with the capability to offer sexual pleasure when properly stimulated. Almost every part of a woman's body has some nerves so as to give maximum sensation during sexual intercourse when stimulated.

However, many married couples are faced with numerous challenges or distracters to having a fruitful and enjoyable sexual experience.

The following are some of the inhibitors to reaching orgasm:

- Lack of concentration

- Uncaring Partner

- Stress

- Depression

- Lack of interest

- Poor planning

- Communication Breakdown

- Lack of knowledge

- Negative attitude toward sex

- Negative thoughts towards sex

In fact, it is almost impossible to compartmentalise sex from other equally important areas of marriage. When you get married you are not immune to pressures of this world. Furthermore, to be productive in marriage you need to utilize your valuable time which is a scarce resource with wisdom, because we have a lot of competing needs that demand our attention.

There is need for married couples to have a holistic approach to sex, because sex is not done in a vacuum. Whatever goes on in a home will eventually affect the quality of sexual relationship of a couple. So it is very important to be considerate to each other as wives and husbands because whatever happens will ultimately have a bearing on our sexual intimacy.

Especially our women fork tend to get easily affected by what goes on in a home. Nevertheless, despite a long list of competing needs, we should endeavor to set aside enough time for sexual intimacy or else the devil will have a field day as we deprive each other of sex.

However, a woman needs enough time of foreplay if she is to experience maximum sexual pleasure. She also needs to get involved fully in lovemaking and the entire process of sexual intercourse. In fact, she must try by all means to avoid passivity and engage herself fully in the whole process of sexual intercourse. Lack of concentration will result in delayed sexual satisfaction. She may not even reach orgasm and the whole sexual process may just end up to be a mere academic exercise which might lead to resentment and frustration.

HOW TO GIVE YOUR WIFE MAXIMUM PLEASURE THROUGH CLITORAL AND G-SPOT STIMULATION

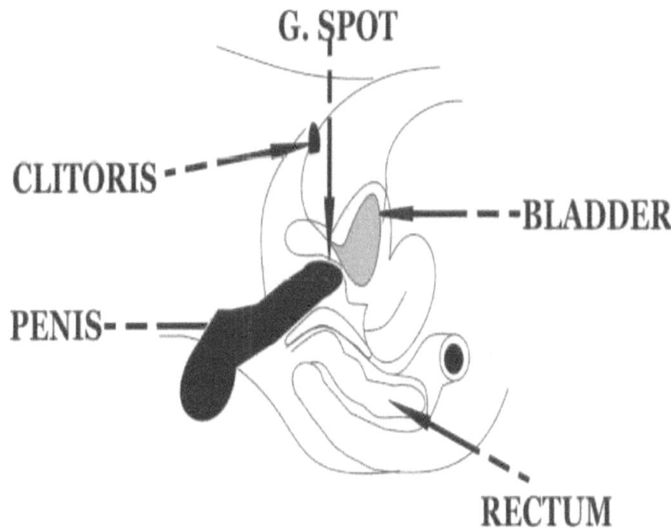

Figure 5: Clitoral and G. Spot Stimulation

CLITORAL STIMULATION

A Clitoris is the most sensitive part of the female sexual organ and the primary source of female sexual pleasure. It can be likened or compared to a penis: It is extremely sensitive to touch, but when properly and gently stimulated it engorges with blood and becomes a source of great pleasure and sexual release to a woman. A romantic and affectionate husband can help his wife reach orgasm as he takes mastery of clitoral stimulation.

G-SPOT STIMULATION

The G-Spot, also popularly known Grafenberg spot (German gynecologist Ernst Grafenberg), is a bean-shaped erogenous area of the vagina. When properly stimulated it leads to strong sexual arousal resulting in powerful orgasms and female ejaculation also known as squirting. G-Spot Orgasm is so powerful such that your woman can shake uncontrollably and squirt with ecstasy.

CHAPTER ELEVEN

VICTORY OVER IMPOTENCE
IN MARRIAGE

CAUSES OF LOW SEX LIBIDO AND
IMPOTENCE IN MEN

The causes of low sex libido and impotence in men could be attributed to many different health challenges. It is actually quite depressing and painful for any man to be found in such a dilemma. There is nothing more painful, frustrating, degrading, and depressing than failing to meet the sexual need of your wife. The ego of a man is completely crashed whenever he fails to satisfy his wife in bed. The pride of every man lays in having a satisfactory sexual encounter with his dear wife. **Therefore, low sex libido or impotence can kill the ego of any man. Actually, for any husband to enjoy sex he has to be in good health and perfect frame of mind. The mind is one of the most powerful organs in the human body that enhances sexual performance in marriage.**

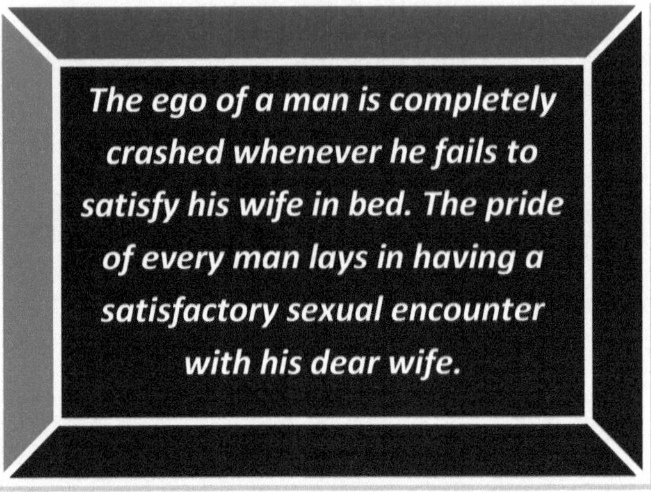

Find below a list of causes of low sex libido and impotence in men.

I. **STRESS:** Stress is pressure or worry caused by problems in somebody's life. When one is stressed it becomes very difficult to relax. It is usually, generated by a number of factors in someone's life.

According to Richard J. B. Willis in his book 'Cracking the Stress Problem', he says the term 'Stress' is borrowed from the world of mechanics and physics where stress is described as, 'the physical pressure exerted upon, and between parts of a body; when deformation occurs as a result it is called "strain". Other physicists and engineers call stress 'the cohesive force of molecular resistance in a body opposing the action of applied external force'. The external force being described in turn as a stressor. He further states that all stress is not harmful. Stressors include basic feelings or urges expressed as, say, hunger, thirst, and tiredness. Without these feelings we would not go looking for food, drink and rest which help to keep our bodies alive, fit and well. Conversely, stress also includes the heart-rending emotional strains of bereavement or divorce, and other long term problems giving rise to persistent or recurring anxieties.'

For instance; Lack of finances to meet basic needs in a home can cause anxiety in marriage. Anxiety caused by thinking of how to satisfy your partner in bed. How to sustain an erection during sex can create a cycle of ongoing erectile dysfunction.

II. **WORKAHOLIC**: A Workaholic man is ever fatigued as a result his sexual drive is negatively affected and causes him to underperform sexually.

III. **MEDICAL CONDITION**: (Diabetes, Heart Conditions or disease) Diabetes, hypertension can certainly cause low sex libido and may lead to impotence in men. These are medications which may include use of prescribed drugs to treat: high blood pressure, heart disease, depression, seizures, and cancers.

IV. NAGGING WIFE: According to the Oxford Dictionary of English the word nag means **to keep complaining to somebody about their behavior or keep asking them to do something.**

Therefore, a nagging wife is a wife who keeps complaining to her husband about his behaviour and keeps asking him to do something.

The most common complaints which married women generally have against their husbands include the following;

i) When the husband ejaculates early during or before sexual intercourse leaving his wife unsatisfied sexually.

ii) When the husband experiences the inability to achieve an erection and therefore unable to have full sex because his manhood or penis is flaccid despite having intense lovemaking. This situation can make a wife explode in anger and lash out at her poor husband in frustration.

iii) When the husband is unable to provide basic needs in a home.

iv) Failure by the husband to give his wife full attention.

v) Failure by the husband to support his family financially.

vi) When the husband is seen not to help with some house chores in a home.

vii) When the husband reaches home late without notifying his wife earlier in the day

viii) When the husband fails to communicate to his wife during the day

A nagging wife can exacerbate the husband's problem of low sex libido and impotence. So a person with erectile dysfunction can be griped with the spirit of fear which can generate feelings of anger, resentment, and frustration leading to low self-esteem. Hence, this condition can create adverse effects on the total wellbeing of the husband. Remember, there is always a better way of expressing your displeasure to your husband. Nagging him will make the situation worse. Hence, think before you utter a word, because it is impossible to reverse your words once uttered. The word of caution for a nagging wife is that learn to use proper channels of communication.

V. **UNFORGIVING:** Lack of forgiveness in marriage can generate feelings of anger, resentment, and frustration. Unforgiving normally creates a barrier between the husband and wife. This barrier makes it impossible to communicate effectively. As long as communication lines are not open, it is almost impossible for the husband to maintain and sustain an erection. When the wife fails to forgive her husband and let go of perceived ill-treatment can keep the husband in bondage and perpetuate erectile dysfunction. For some reasons, it is often not unusual for married couples to easily misunderstand each other, at times over trivial issues. Men and women are completely different from each other. We differ in many ways: in the manner we talk, eat, laugh, cry, reason, think, dress, and in many other aspects of life. Although we differ in many ways, the things that unite us are greater than the things that divide us. Stereotype is a cancer that puts the life of our spouse on the line. Both men and women should endeavor to knowledgeably understand each other. We need to complement each other.

VI.   **OBESITY:** Men who are obese have a higher risk of suffering from erectile dysfunction than men who are not. According to an online article of Harvard Health Publishing **(HARVARD MEDICAL SCHOOL)** of March, 2011, and I quote, **"Although men with erectile dysfunction (ED) often blame testosterone, hormonal disorders account for only 3% of erectile dysfunction. But even with normal testosterone levels, men who are obese have an increased risk of erectile dysfunction"**. For example, a Harvard study found that a man with a 42-inch waist is as twice as likely to develop the problem as a gent with a 32-inch waist. Brazilian research also linked abdominal obesity to erectile dysfunction, but only in men older than 60. And a California study reported that having a BMI of 28 (overweight but not obese) increased a man's odds of developing erectile dysfunction by over 90%.

Establishing a link is one thing; finding a way to improve erectile function, another. But a Massachusetts study found that weight loss can indeed improve things for overweight men with erectile dysfunction. Similar results were reported by Italian scientists who randomly assigned 110 obese men with erectile dysfunction to a diet and exercise program or to simply continue their usual care. After two years, more than 30% of the men in the diet and exercise group had corrected their erectile dysfunction without medication, compared with less than 6% in the group that received their usual level of medical care. Men who lost the most weight enjoyed the greatest benefit." www.health.harvard.edu

VII. **GUILTY:** Infidelity or unfaithfulness can generate guilty feelings in a man which in turn immobilize his sexual ability. When a husband is promiscuous he can be haunted by guilty feelings of sin and shame which can lead to erectile dysfunction.

VIII.   **ALCOHOL:** Is a depressant, and when taken heavily can dampen mood, decrease sexual desire, and make it difficult for a man to achieve erection

IX.   **CIGARETTE SMOKING**: According to an online article published by a BBC's Health Correspondent Richard Hannaford, "A study found that smokers were twice as likely to become impotent". The same process by which smoking causes heart disease is responsible for impotence. Atherosclerosis, or hardening of the arteries, can narrow the smaller blood vessels leading to the penis. In addition, nicotine makes blood vessels into and out of the penis narrow still further. While this effect stops immediately the man quits smoking, the arterial hardening takes some time to reverse.

It is recommended to keep away from cigarette smoking because it can damage the blood vessels and hinder proper blood flow. ED or impotence is as a result of poor arteries that supply blood to the penis.

X.   **INSOMNIA:** Is a condition of being unable to sleep. This condition if left unchecked can cause low sex drive and Erectile Dysfunction. According to an online guest post on www.psychologytoday.com, dated 22 August, 2018, by **Chris Brantner,** certified Sleep Science Coach and founder of SleepZoo.com, subtitled, "How Short Sleep Negatively Impacts our Sex Lives:

Anxiety and depression, both side effects of insomnia and sleep deprivation, are known to cause sexual dysfunction for a variety of reasons, both physical and cognitive. When the body becomes stressed due to lack of sleep, the brain suppresses production of sex hormones like estrogen and testosterone in favour of stress hormones like cortisol. This shift in hormone levels can lead to decreased sex drive, infertility, or erectile dysfunction.

Research has shown that sex before bed can help improve sleep quality thanks to the endorphins released by sex, which serve to ease anxiety and relax you. And all of that great sleep can actually subsequently improve your relationship with your significant other. Sex also releases oxytocin, a hormone known as the "love hormone," which has numerous benefits to your body and mind, including cueing relaxation.

In order to ensure your body is ready for sex, follow the National Sleep Foundation's guidelines and shoot for between 7 and 8 hours sleep each night."

TREATMENT OF
IMPOTENCE

Impotence is defined as, not potent: lacking in power, strength, or vigor: helpless. Unable to engage in sexual intercourse because of inability to have and maintain an erection broadly: sterile. www.merriam-webster.com. Impotence or Erectile dysfunction is the inability to get and keep an erection firm enough for sex.

The word impotence is derived from the Latin word impotencia, which literally translated means lack of power.

Natural means are the best ways of treatment of impotence. However, find below some other ways in which impotence can treated.

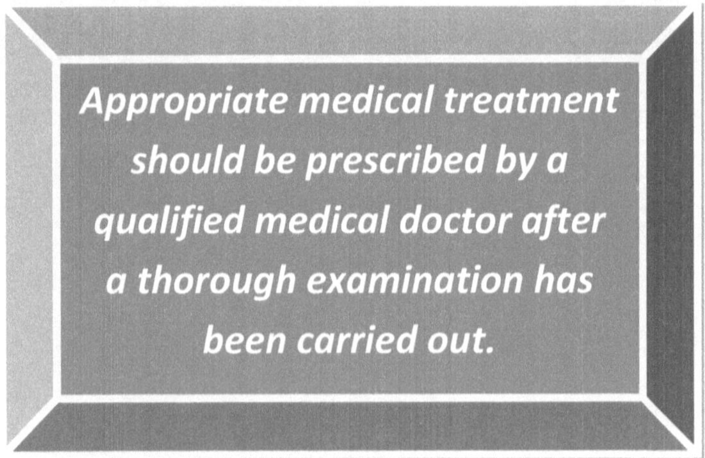

1.) VASODILATOR

YOHIMBINE: It is used for the treatment of organic impotence, in particular with patients with diabetes. Yohimbine can cause dilation of peripheral blood vessels along with the central nervous system stimulation. Some side effects associated with its use are dizziness, stomach upset and dry mouth.

2.) VACUUM THERAPY

A vacuum Constriction Device (VCD): It is an external pump with a band on it that a man with erectile dysfunction can use to get and maintain an erection. The VCD has an Acrylic cylinder with a pump that may be attached directly to the end of the penis. But using one too often or too long can damage elastic tissue in the penis, consequently less firm erections will be the result.

3.) PENILE INJECTION DRUGS

- **ALPROSTADIL (Caverject, Edex, Muse):** It is injected as a solution directly into the penis several minutes before having sex. It can be used up to three times per week. Common side effects of this drug include redness and irritation at the injection area.

- **Avanafil (Stendra):** This is an oral drug taken fifteen minutes before having sex once per day. Avoid taking nitrates with this drug because it can cause severely low blood pressure and even death. Common side effects of this drug include headache, flushing (reddening of the face), low blood pressure, blurry vision (changes in how red and green look)hearing (Tinnitus-ringing in the ear) sounds are heard differently.

- **Sildenafil (Viagra):** Is used as an oral drug in tablet form, taken only once per day, and an hour before sex. The common side effects include headache, flushing, stomach upset, vision changes.

- **Tadalafil (Cialis):** Is used as an oral drug that increases blood flow throughout the body, taken thirty 30 minutes before sex and may work up to 48 hours. The common side effects include headache, nausea, flushing, stomach upset, and vision changes.

- **Testosterone:** It is the main sex hormone in the male body. It comes in many forms. Naturally, testosterone levels drop with age and this can bring about issues such as erectile dysfunction, low sex libido, a reduction in sperm count, and an increase in weight. If not properly administered could lead to heart attack or stroke. The common side effects include acne, breasts or prostate growth, swelling caused by fluid retention, moodiness, sleep apnea (interrupted breathing during sleep)

4.) PENILE IMPLANTATION/PROSTHESIS

- **Penile implantation/prosthesis:** Is a medical device which is surgically implanted within the corpora cavernosa of the penis. This device helps the man achieve an erection and regain sexual function. This is usually done when men with erectile dysfunction fail to respond to other types of treatments.

  Find below the three types of penile implant;

  - A Pair Of Malleable Rods

  - A Self–Contained Pair Of Inflatable Prosthetic Cylinders

  - A Three-Piece Fully Inflatable Prosthesis

5.) PENILE REVASCULARISATION

Also known as microvascular arterial bypass surgery for impotence, similar to a cardiac bypass. The main aim of this surgery is to restore proper blood flow to the penis by bypassing the blocked artery.

TIPS ON HOW TO PREVENT ERECTILE DYSFUNCTION

- Watch what you eat

  Some of the best foods that will boost your libido are as follows: Watermelon, Almonds, Avocados, strawberries and raspberries, Walnuts, Chocolates, Eggs, Peaches, Coffee, Saffron and steak.

- Maintain a healthy weight: **A normal healthy weight is Body Mass Index (BMI) between 18.5 and 24.9**

  BMI=Your Weight (in Pounds) x 703 divided by your height (in inches) squared

  Normal Weight = 18.5 to 24.9

  Overweight = 25.0 to 29.9

  Underweight = under 18.5

- Avoid high blood pressure cholesterol

- Avoid drinking alcohol

- Avoid anabolic steroids

- Exercise regularly

- Maintain a healthy lifestyle

WHEN A COUPLE FACES THE STORM OF IMPOTENCE

When a married man who once was virile suddenly loses the power to keep an erection firm enough to have sex, it becomes unbearable not only for him, but also his wife as well. The first reaction of the wife is feeling rejection and taking the blame. The wife would blame herself for his inability to have an erection. She might think that she is not doing enough to help her husband achieve an erection. A lot of negative thoughts would be crossing her mind, accusing her of being cold and passive during sex. Sadly, these thoughts would generate the spirit of rejection and self-condemnation in her heart.

Alternatively, she would respond with hostility and resentment towards her husband. She might start suspecting him of having an extra marital affair. Without seeking Godly counsel the wife might also be tempted to having an extra marital affair. Otherwise, if not handled with wisdom the marriage can end in divorce. However, during this difficult time it would be prudent for the couple to employ the lines of communication effectively to better handle the matter with wisdom and understanding. Discard all thoughts of self-condemnation, hostility towards each other and allow your husband to feel free to talk to you and share his fears and concerns.

SEEK MEDICAL AND SPIRITUAL HELP

Especially, the husband should be bold enough to quickly seek medical help from a qualified doctor. The wife should encourage her husband to see a medical doctor and seek spiritual counsel from a qualified godly marriage counselor. She should also be readily available to offer moral and spiritual support to her husband.

Please Note: No content in this book, regardless of date, should ever be used as a substitute for direct medical advice from your doctor or other qualified clinician.

In conclusion, allow me to state that true love and sexual intimacy in marriage can become a reality if you choose to love your mate as you love yourself. Love your spouse with all your heart. Love cannot be love without upholding the seven characteristics of true love; commitment, selflessness, sacrifice, discipline, patience, kindness and forgiveness. When you uphold these virtues and values in your marriage everything else will fall in place.

Don't despair or throw in the towel, but endeavour to assimilate the liberating insights from this book and be transformed into the perfect couple as God originally designed you to be. God originally designed you in such a manner that once you love your mate wholeheartedly, then with the same measure of love that you exhibit towards your spouse it will also be expressed to you pressed down, shaken together shall your spouse give that love to you. When you learn to practice true love sexual intimacy will become easy. The ultimate sexual intimacy in marriage is the product of true love. True love is always expressed through sexual intimacy as the ultimate pleasure and fulfillment a couple can ever have.

The Holy Bible in the book of **Romans 12:1-2**, *says,*

"I beseech you therefore, brethren, by the mercies of God, that you present your bodies a living sacrifice, holy, acceptable to God, which is your reasonable service."

And do not be conformed to this world, but be transformed by the renewing of your mind, that you may prove what is that good and acceptable and perfect will of God.

My prayer is that true love shall characterise your marriage. May God cause your marriage to flourish and be productive! May He bless your marriage with true love and cause you to experience the ultimate sexual intimacy. May your marriage experience a great transformation by the renewal of your mind! May you walk and experience that good and perfect will of God for your marriage.

GLOSSARY

- **TESTOSTERONE:** It is the main sex hormone in the male body. It comes in many forms. naturally, testosterone levels drop with age and this can bring about issues such as erectile dysfunction, low sex libido, a reduction in sperm count, and an increase in weight.

- **LIBIDO:** Sexual appetite, sexual passion, sexual urge, sexual longing, sexual desire.

- **VASODILATOR:** It is used for the treatment of organic impotence, in particular with patients with diabetes. yohimbine can cause dilation of peripheral blood vessels along with the central nervous system stimulation. some side effects associated with its use are dizziness, stomach upset and dry mouth.

- **VACUUM THERAPY:** A vacuum constriction device (VCD): It is an external pump with a band on it.

- **IMPOTENCE:** It's not potent: lacking in power, strength, or vigor: helpless, unable to engage in sexual intercourse because of inability to have and maintain an erection broadly: sterile.

- **SILDENAFIL (VIAGRA):** Is used as an oral drug in tablet form, taken only once per day, and an hour before sex. the common side effects include headache, flushing, stomach upset, vision changes.

- **TADALAFIL:** (Cialis): Is used as an oral drug that increases blood flow throughout the body, taken thirty 30 minutes before sex and may work up to 48 hours. the common side effects include headache, nausea, flushing, stomach upset, and vision changes.

- **PENILE IMPLANTATION/PROSTHESIS:** Is a medical device which is surgically implanted within the corpora cavernosa of the penis. this device helps the man achieve an erection and regain sexual function. this is usually done when men with erectile dysfunction fail to respond to other types of treatments.

- **INSOMNIA:** Is a condition of being unable to sleep. this condition if left unchecked can cause low sex drive and erectile dysfunction.

- **ALPROSTADIL** (caverject, edex, muse): It is injected as a solution directly into the penis several minutes before having sex. it can be used up to three times per week. common side effects of this drug include redness and irritation at the injection area.

- **The G-SPOT**, also popularly known Grafenberg spot (German gynecologist Ernst Grafenberg).

- **ORGASM:** An orgasm is the climax or peak of sexual excitement, during the sexual response cycle, characterized by intensely pleasurable and sensational feelings around the genital area.

- **GAY:** Is defined as a man having unnatural sexual or physical activity with a fellow man, in which they touch each other's sexual organs, and which may include anal sex.

- **LESBIAN:** Is defined as a woman having unnatural sexual or physical activity with a fellow woman, in which they touch each other's sexual organs.

- **FORGIVENESS:** Is the act of forgiving. To forgive is to cease to feel resentment against an offender.

- **KINDNESS:** Is the ability or quality of being gentle and considerate of other people's feelings and wellbeing. It is treating people with respect and dignity.

- **DISCIPLINE:** Is defined as control gained by enforcing obedience or order.

- **PATIENCE:** Is the ability to remain calm and not become agitated or annoyed when your expectations are delayed.

- **SACRIFICE:** Sacrifice is giving up something of value or importance to you in order to get or pursue something that seems more important and of great value.

- **COMMITMENT:** Commitment is to be completely loyal to a person or spouse, a thing and pledge to devote all your time and effort to fulfilling set objectives and plans.

- **DEFRAUD:** Means to deprive of something by deception.

- **SEMINAL VESICLES:** The seminal Vesicles are two small organs located below the bladder. They produce semen which is the fluid that sperm moves around in.

- **PROSTATE GLAND:** The prostate gland is the size of a walnut or golf ball and is located between the bladder and the penis. It is actually in front of the rectum.

- **COWPER'S GLANDS:** The Cowper's gland produces a fluid called pre-ejaculate. This fluid prepares the urethra for ejaculation. It reduces friction so the semen can move more easily. The Cowper's glands are under the prostate and attach to the urethra. They are also called bulbourethral glands.

- **URETHRA:** The urethra is the tube that carries urine from the bladder to the outside of the body

- **CREMASTER:** It is a thin muscle consisting of loops of fibers derived from the internal oblique muscle and descending upon the spermatic cord to surround and suspend the testicle.

- **URETHRA:** The urethral opening is located just below the clitoris and it is the tiny hole that is used to pee urine out of the bladder

- **.VAGINA:** The vaginal opening is located just below the urethral opening. This is the passage where menstrual blood leaves the body, and it is also where babies are born through.

- **ANUS:** The anus is the opening to the rectum. It has a lot of sensitive nerve endings. According to God's design its sole purpose is to excrete waste matters from the body. Therefore, it is morally very wrong for some people to use it for sexual pleasure.

- **MONS PUBIS:** The mons pubis is the fleshy mound above the vulva. Generally, after puberty pubic hair starts to grow around this area. Its main function is to cushion the pubic bone.

- **VAGINA:** The vagina is a tube connecting the vulva (outer part of the vagina) with the cervix and uterus (inner parts of the vagina).The vagina is really stretchy and expands when aroused.

- **CERVIX:** The cervix is located between the vagina and the uterus. It has an opening connecting the vagina and the uterus. It allows the menstrual blood out of the uterus, and also allows the sperm into the uterus. The cervix stretches open or dilates during childbirth.

  One can actually feel the cervix when a penis or any other object is inserted into the vagina.

- **UTERUS:** The uterus is a muscular organ shaped like a pear and about the size of a small fist. It is often called the womb because it is where a fetus grows during pregnancy. Usually the lower part of the uterus lifts toward the belly button when sexually aroused. This is the reason why the vagina stretches or gets longer when aroused sexually.

- **FALLOPIAN TUBES:** These are two narrow tubes that carry eggs from the ovaries to the uterus. It is also a passage where sperm moves through to fertilize the egg.

- **FIMBRIAE:** The fimbriae look like tiny fingers at the end of each fallopian tube. When the ovary releases an egg, they help sweep it into the fallopian tube.

- **OVARIES:** The ovaries are used to store the eggs and they also produce hormones such as estrogen, progesterone, and testosterone. These hormones usually help to regulate menstrual cycles and pregnancy. It is during puberty that the ovaries start to release an egg each month until menopause. Sometimes more than one egg is released in a month.

- **BARTHOLIN'S GLANDS:** These are located near the vaginal opening. They often release fluid that lubricate the vagina when one is aroused sexually.

- **SKENE'S GLANDS:** The Skene's glands are located on either side of the urethral opening. They secrete or release fluid during female ejaculation. They are also called paraurethral glands or female prostate glands.

- **HYMEN:** The hymen is the thin fleshy tissue that covers or stretches across part of the opening to the vagina.

214

BIBLIOGRAPHY

- Urinary Stress Incontinence, Dr. Arnold H. Kegel, strengthening the Pubucoccygeus (P. C.) muscle

- Cracking The Stress Problem, J. B. Willis, Richard

- The Joy of Committed Love, Smalley Gary

- Article on Cigarette Smoking, Hannaford Richard

- Insomnia, Brantner, Chris. certified Sleep Science Coach and founder of SleepZoo.com, Source: www.psychologytoday.com

- Obesity: online article of Harvard Health Publishing.

- Third Edition, Intended for Pleasure, by Ed Wheat, M. D. and Gaye Wheat

- The Key Ingredients to Success by Bishop Dr. Joe Imakando

- Why Do Guys Get Sleepy After Sex?' by Melinda Wenner of Scienceline, www.livescience.com

- www.healthline.com

- www.merriamwebster.com

- www.https://en.wikipedia.org/wiki/Levator_ani

- William H. Masters and Virginia E. Johnson (1915 – 2001), and 1925)

- http://onlinelibrary.wiley.com

ABOUT THE AUTHOR

Jossy Phiri is a born again Christian who serves as an Elder and Marriage Counselor at Bread of Life Church International, under the able leadership of his grace **Bishop Dr. Joe Imakando**, the founder, President and overseer. Phiri holds two bachelor's Degrees, a Bachelor's Degree in Ministry Honours and Bachelor's Degree in Christian Entrepreneurship from Team Impact Christian University of 8894 Airline Hwy Suite E Baton Rouge, LA 70815, USA.

He and his beloved wife **Veronica** have been married for 27 years and together have four beautiful children, namely; **Hannah, Joshua, Caleb** and **Emmanuel** .